WE DO LANGUAGE

English Language Variation in the Secondary English Classroom

WE DO LANGUAGE

English Language Variation in the Secondary English Classroom

Anne H. Charity Hudley
Christine Mallinson

Foreword by Jacqueline Jones Royster

Teachers College, Columbia University
New York and London

Published by Teachers College Press, 1234 Amsterdam Avenue, New York, NY 10027

Library of Congress Cataloging-in-Publication Data

Charity Hudley, Anne H.
We Do Language: English language variation in the secondary English classroom/ Anne H. Charity Hudley; Christine Mallinson; Foreword by Jacqueline Jones Royster.
pages cm
Includes bibliographical references and index.
ISBN 978-0-8077-5498-6 (pbk.)—ISBN 978-0-8077-5499-3 (hardcover)
1. English language—Variation. 2. Second language acquisition—Study and teaching. 3. Classroom environment—Social aspects. 4. English language—Study and teaching—Foreign speakers. I. Title. II. Title: English language variation in the secondary English classroom.
PE1074.7.C53 2014
427—dc23
2013029277

ISBN 978-0-8077-5498-6 (paper)
ISBN 978-0-8077-5499-3 (hardcover)
eISBN 978-0-8077-7251-5 (ebook)

Printed on acid-free paper

Manufactured in the United States of America

21 20 19 18 17 16 15 14 8 7 6 5 4 3 2 1

Contents

Foreword

In the first decades of the 21st century, we are living in an era when peace does not prevail and in a world in which cross-cultural complexities and tensions are palpable from nation to nation around the globe. We have, however, worlds within this world where, often amid difficult conditions and circumstances, teachers continue to have the responsibility of preparing current and future youth to assume their places as capable citizens and leaders. A primary piece of that responsibility in the United States lies in the hands of English/language arts professionals. We must rise to this critical occasion and be as careful, conscientious, and innovative as we can while we think through the intricate connections among languages, literacies, histories, and cultures and the designing of learning experiences that are innovative and enabling of success. For new generations of students, success is linked to the multiple ways in which they will be called upon to be global citizens, capable of functioning respectfully across cultural and national boundaries while also working well as communicators, workers, and leaders within the company of others who are both alike and different from themselves.

Anne H. Charity Hudley and Christine Mallinson have taken this basic charge quite seriously. In *We Do Language: English Language Variation in the Secondary English Classroom*, they have penned a volume that lays out in an accessible, pragmatic, and adaptable way the thorny problem space that secondary English/language arts professionals face as they do their jobs—with intentionality and dedication—in classrooms that are multiply defined by socioeconomic status, culture, gender, sexuality, ideology, and other vectors of the human condition and experience. Drawing together a richly articulated and manageable array of theoretical principles and pedagogical frameworks about language, literacy, and culture, Charity Hudley and Mallinson connect these principles and frameworks to action. *We Do Language* is grounded in specific examples of the work that teachers and students are actually doing and exemplifying. As the book title suggests, the primary goal of their research is to investigate what success looks like when educators and students actually "do language." The anticipated outcome of this effort is their hope that this book will be a valuable resource in helping teachers build knowledge, insight, workable teaching/learning strategies, and academic impact related to

- the nature of language and how our uses of it have the capacity to vary in context, content, purpose, mode, and medium;
- language, literature, and other texts as operational tools within communicative and cultural contexts, and how fluency and flexibility with these tools become critical skills as students develop linguistic and cultural knowledge and sharpen a critical aesthetic for understanding the impact of language and culture as sociopolitical phenomena;
- the interface of orality and literacy, with particular regard for how texts of various kinds function, not only within traditions of creative expressiveness, but also as "artifacts" of the languages, cultures, and communities in which they are produced; and
- the dynamic intersections between building linguistic knowledge and building cultural knowledge as we all work in common cause to prepare students well as consumers, producers, and leaders in whatever postsecondary school worlds the students may enter.

I found the authors' discussion of macro- and microcultures, and the extent to which these cultures do and do not intersect, to be particularly useful in a two-fold way. On one hand, Charity Hudley and Mallinson offer a different paradigm for helping students to think more substantively about language variation not as jargon but rather as a paradigmatic anchor or an enabling lens for understanding human behavior, interaction, and performance within their own lives and actions. On the other hand, they offer a springboard, strengthened by a broader and deeper accountability of the human enterprise more globally rendered, from which teachers might enhance their capacity to generate innovative and meaningful activities for students as authorized and authentic linguistic investigators. I find the paradigm of students as linguistic investigators to be compelling. By interrogating and integrating students' own lives and practices within the company of various others, this approach has the capacity to open clearer pathways for understanding and performance. Such experimentations carry the promise of enabling a more visceral on-the-ground sense of the ways and means of human diversity, not simply as an interesting concept, but as dynamic action. As a resource, *We Do Language* encourages teachers and students to till the ground of their understanding of language and culture as human phenomena so that they can pay more critical attention to what both diversity and complexity actually mean and thereby enhance their capacity to function as astute language users going forward.

The question that Charity Hudley and Mallinson encourage us to consider is how linguistic and cultural knowledge endow the potential for transitioning from active learning about language, literacy, and culture to the active use of this knowledge as language producers and cultural interlocutors in various micro- and macrocultural contexts, especially as students move beyond school to the world of work or to colleges and universities for professional preparation. The critical assumption is that knowledge informs creativity and productivity as students experiment in high school classrooms with various modalities and digital technologies and enhance their capacity to exercise linguistic agency—flexibly, effectively, efficiently, and ethically in speaking, writing, reading, critical thinking, and problem solving.

As a linguist by training, I am very much intrigued by Charity Hudley's and Mallinson's enthusiasm for a linguistically informed approach. I share that enthusiasm and have functioned over my career as a researcher and teacher with these same values. However, I suspect that the real news in this volume is likely to be the extent to which the authors have documented a linkage of this theoretical knowledge to a growing body of pedagogical work that emanates from these theoretical frames. I find myself most intrigued by the stories of success that they share from the teachers whom they have interviewed for this volume and by the potential of these accounts to engender a much-needed discussion for educational reform in English/language arts. *We Do Language* is a theoretically well-grounded resource that is also accessible, practical, and adaptable as a tool for bringing success more deliberately to scale, and offers a provocative and invaluable paradigm for this process. This book is an enabling tool for helping teachers and those who prepare them to face—perhaps better than we ever have—the challenge of schooling in the English/language arts for the 21st century.

Jacqueline Jones Royster
Ivan Allen Chair in Liberal Arts and Technology and Dean
Ivan Allen College of Liberal Arts
Georgia Institute of Technology

Preface

WHEN AUTHOR AND PROFESSOR Toni Morrison gave the Nobel Lecture after accepting the Nobel Prize for Literature in 1993, she explained the centrality of language to our daily lives: "We die. That may be the meaning of life," Morrison said. "But we do language. That may be the measure of our lives" (Morrison, 1993).

Language is a nuanced, complex social tool that is used in different ways and in different contexts, as we are all culturally and linguistically diverse speakers. In this book, we investigate how educators and students "do language" in diverse ways within secondary English classrooms. We examine the complexities of how educators and students communicate with one another as well as understand what is being communicated by the authors whose novels, plays, poems, and other texts are commonly read in secondary English classrooms.

We believe that knowledge about language, language variation, culture, and communication is critical to the mission of helping all students achieve in the secondary English classroom. Throughout this book, concepts, skills, strategies, activities, models, and vignettes developed by us and by other teachers show how to integrate and apply information about English language variation to secondary English classrooms. By developing insight into and appreciation for the nuances of language, by learning to communicate effectively, and by working to understand diverse modes of expression, students acquire and hone the linguistic skills that are not only central to academic advancement but that are also valued in our multicultural society.

Acknowledgments

How lovely it is, this thing we have done—together.
Toni Morrison (1993)

ABOVE ALL, WE THANK our families. Anne writes this book in honor of Cynthia and Renard Charity and in memory of Alfred and Sarah Charity and Leslie and Annie McClennon (who was a secondary English educator). Special thanks to J. Chris Hudley; Renée Charity Price and Mike, Carter, and Caroline Price; and Renard Jr., Madeleine, Emma, and Olivia Charity. Thanks also to the Hudley family, most of all Marie, Jay, and Tiffaney Hudley.

Christine writes this book in honor of Talia Mallinson and in memory of Karl and Anna Hoffmann. Special thanks to Josh Birenbaum, Jim and Carla Mallinson, Stephen Mallinson, and Melanie Luques.

We owe immense debts of gratitude to our mentors and teachers: William Labov and Walt Wolfram, first and foremost, as well as Carolyn Temple Adger, Connie Eble, Darion Griffin, Lee Perkins, John Shelton Reed, John Rickford, Hollis Scarborough, and the late Calvert Watkins. Without each of you, we would not be the scholars we are today.

We thank everyone who has worked with us at Teachers College Press. We are especially indebted to our editors Brian Ellerbeck and Meg Hartmann; to Nancy Power and Emily Renwick for marketing assistance; and to James A. Banks for support and encouragement. To be able to work with Teachers College Press on two books has been a privilege and a real pleasure. We are further indebted to our manuscript reviewers, who gave us excellent feedback that improved this book, and to Melissa Hogarty, who helped us with proofreading and editing. We also acknowledge Dana Dillehunt, who took Christine's photograph for this book, and Stephen Salpukas, who took Anne's photograph.

We offer heartfelt thanks to each of the educators who contributed vignettes to this book: Dr. Mary Bucholtz, Dr. Catherine Evans Davies, Ruth Harper, Brian Higginson, Julie Hildbold, Christopher Justice, Linda Krause, April Lawrence, Kerrigan Mahoney, Jessica Medina, Dr. Lisa Cohen Minnick, Dr. Jeffrey Reaser, Dr. Elaine Richardson, Julie Roos, Jessica Shildt,

Clare Trow, Ashleigh Greene Wade, Blake Williams, Cleveland Winfield, and Mario Zangla. It is far better for having incorporated your insights and voices! We also thank our wonderful colleagues—many of whom are current or former inservice educators—who read entire drafts of this book and shared invaluable advice and suggestions: Phillip Carter, Stephany Dunstan, Christopher Justice, Lynn Moore, Nancy Shelton, Laura Strickling, and Cleveland Winfield.

We especially thank the educators who attended our 2009 and 2010 summer workshops at Virginia Commonwealth University and our 2010–2013 workshops with Baltimore City Public Schools and with Middle Grades Partnership. We learned so much from hearing what each of you had to say. These workshops would not have been possible without the inspirational leadership of Beth Drummond Casey, Amy Rosenkrans, and Dr. Sonja Brookins Santelises.

We appreciate the feedback, assistance, and encouragement that we received from other scholars and friends, many of whom read and listened to sections of this book manuscript, including Sara Brandt, Jessica Calarco, De Ferenbach, Katie Ford, Monica Griffin, Jenny Hindman, Gay Ivey, Denise Johnson, John Moore, Gail Orgelfinger, Abena Osseo-Asare, Lynn Pelco, Jeffrey Reaser, Jan Rozelle, Gillian Sankoff, and Ben Torbert.

We recognize our colleagues at the College of William & Mary and the University of Maryland–Baltimore County (UMBC), particularly our deans and department chairs, who were instrumental in providing us with research leaves so that we could complete this project. We especially thank the School-University Research Network (SURN), led by Jan Rozzelle, and all of the Virginia school leaders and educators who participated in the Capstone English Project, the Senior English Seminar Academy, and the College & Career Readiness Initiatives from 2011 to the present. We also thank former colleagues, professors, and mentors at Dartmouth University, Harvard University, North Carolina State University, the University of North Carolina at Chapel Hill, and the University of Pennsylvania.

Our current and former students have been a great resource. Special thanks to Christine's research assistant, Holly Britton, and to our doctoral student mentees Inte'a DeShields, Hannah Askin Franz, April Lawrence, and Kerrigan Mahoney, who have also been secondary English educators. We also acknowledge Anne's undergraduate students Brittney Calloway, Jerome Carter, Morgan Figa, Rachel Granata, Will Morris, Bailey Rose, and Kenay Sudler, as well as all of the students in Anne's courses "African American English," "American Speech," "Introduction to Community Studies," and "Language Attitudes," and students in Christine's courses "Language in Diverse Schools and Communities" and "Language Variation and Education."

We have presented material from this book at various conferences, including the American Dialect Society (2010), American Educational Research Association (2012), American Federation of Teachers (2011), ASCD (2012), College English Association (2012), International Reading Association (2011), Linguistic Society of America (2013), National Association of Independent Schools People of Color (2011), National Association for Multicultural Education (2010), National Council of Teachers of English (2011, 2012), National Partnership for Educational Access (2012), New Ways of Analyzing Variation (2011, 2013), SouthEastern Conference on Linguistics (2009, 2011, 2013), SETESOL (2011), and Tidewater Math Day (2012).

We also benefited from colleagues and students who gave us their feedback on material from this book at talks given at American University; Coastal Carolina University; the College of William & Mary; Community College of Baltimore County; George Mason University; Georgetown University; James Madison University; Johns Hopkins University; Kansas State University; Notre Dame of Maryland University; Queen Mary, University of London; Stanford University; UMBC; University of Illinois at Chicago; University of Michigan at Ann Arbor; Virginia Commonwealth University; and Virginia State University.

Parts of this book draw upon or are adapted from material we have published elsewhere. We acknowledge Anne's chapters "Linguistics and Social Activism" (Charity Hudley, 2013a), "Sociolinguistic Engagement in Schools: Collecting and Sharing Data" (Charity Hudley, 2013b), and "Teaching About English Language Variations" (Charity Hudley, 2012), as well as Christine's chapter "Interdisciplinary Approaches" (Mallinson & Kendall, 2013) and her chapters in the coedited volume, *Data Collection in Sociolinguistics: Methods and Applications* (Mallinson, Childs, & Van Herk, 2013). We also draw from our coauthored book, *Understanding English Language Variation in U.S. Schools* (Charity Hudley & Mallinson, 2011), and our coauthored articles, "Communicating About Communication: Multidisciplinary Approaches to Educating Educators About Language Variation" (Mallinson & Charity Hudley, 2010) and "A Conceptual Framework for Promoting Linguistic and Educational Change" (Mallinson, Charity Hudley, Strickling, & Figa, 2011).

Our work has been supported by various funding sources. Anne acknowledges the National Science Foundation for BCS-0115676, SES-0512005, and SES-0930522; the State Council of Higher Education in Virginia (SCHEV) Capstone English Project, Senior English Academy, and Visible Leaders grants; the QEP Mellon Initiative at the College of William & Mary; and the College of William & Mary Community Studies Professorship. Anne's research has also been supported in part by a Ford

Foundation Diversity Dissertation Fellowship, grant HD01994 from the National Institute of Child Health and Human Development to Haskins Laboratories, grant R215U990010 from the U.S. Department of Education Office of Educational Research and Improvement to the American Federation of Teachers, and grant H325T090009 from the U.S. Department of Education Office of Special Education Programs. Christine acknowledges the National Science Foundation for BCS-0236838 and BCS-1050938, the UMBC Special Research Assistantship/Initiative Support and Summer Faculty Fellowship, and a course-initiative grant from the UMBC Alex Brown Center for Entrepreneurship.

Our deepest thanks go to the individuals, organizations, and institutions we have mentioned and any we have inadvertently omitted. We are truly grateful for your support.

CHAPTER 1

Doing Language

WE DO LANGUAGE every day, in our personal and our professional lives, when we communicate, when we engage with others, and when we express our cultural backgrounds, our identities, and ourselves. In our multicultural society, including our complex school and classroom settings, we don't all do language in the same ways. Educators and students come from diverse linguistic backgrounds and may speak, read, and write in ways that vary from person to person and group to group. Throughout this book, we consider how educators and students communicate. How can we have conversations about language and language variation? What happens when communication breakdowns occur? How can educators affirm students' linguistic and cultural backgrounds while meeting pedagogical goals?

Many celebrated literary works that are taught in secondary English classrooms showcase linguistic and cultural diversity. Educators may wonder how best to teach about the language variation that appears in literature, while instructing students to master the norms and conventions of standardized English. What can the use of standardized English convey compared to the use of nonstandardized varieties of English? Would Mark Twain's *Adventures of Huckleberry Finn* or Toni Morrison's *The Bluest Eye* speak to readers as effectively if they had been written in standardized English? How can educators and students engage in linguistically and culturally informed discussions and analyses of texts that incorporate language variation?

These are some of the issues and questions we address in this book, in which we present specific concepts, skills, strategies, and models for applying information about language variation to secondary English classrooms. In our previous book, *Understanding English Language Variation in U.S. Schools* (Charity Hudley & Mallinson, 2011), we examined language variation, particularly Southern and African American varieties, and we analyzed the relationship between language variation and educational achievement for culturally and linguistically diverse students. In this book, we respond to the many secondary English educators who asked us to share ideas for how to integrate linguistic knowledge into secondary English classrooms.

We provide topics and questions for linguistic reflection and discussion, as well as exercises that connect material about language variation to curricula and pedagogical practice. While much of the material in this book discusses English language variation in general, we also focus on the linguistic and literary traditions that are emblematic of our own Southern and African American home communities. Finally, in shaded boxes, we share vignettes written by secondary English educators that describe their personal experiences with language variation and explain how they have applied concepts from our book in their own teaching.

This book is not only geared toward secondary English educators. It is also appropriate for anyone interested in learning about the role of language in students' educational experiences in secondary environments and extending to college. Thus, our readership includes language arts and English education practitioners, speech-language pathologists, reading/literacy specialists, guidance counselors, school administrators, parents, guardians, and students themselves.

WHAT SECONDARY ENGLISH EDUCATORS WANT TO KNOW ABOUT LANGUAGE VARIATION

A few months after participating in one of our workshops on language variation, "Marie"—an educator for 17 years who has taught art, technology, special education, and reading, and who has been a school librarian—said,

> Knowledge about language variation enlightened me about our kids and how their language is perceived. I never really thought about it before. It kind of opened my eyes about how there is language variation that I was just not aware of. What I want to learn more about is how to incorporate it, how to get this information across to students who are different from ones I've taught in the past.

Language is not just a theoretical concept, but rather is something that educators and students *do*, routinely and daily. For educators such as Marie, who have learned that understanding linguistic and cultural complexities is critically important, there is an eagerness to apply this information to their own class settings.

We have worked with hundreds of educators like Marie across the United States, through classes and workshops on English language variation in education. In Maryland, one of the organizations we work with is Middle Grades Partnership, which offers academically promising Baltimore middle school students comprehensive summer and after-school learning opportunities, led by master educators in public and independent schools. In Virginia, one of our main partnership organizations is the School-University Research Network (SURN), which began in 1993 as a partnership of the School of Education at the College of William & Mary with 27 Virginia school districts. One of SURN's primary initiatives is the Capstone English Academy, funded by the Virginia Department of Education and the State Council of Higher Education for Virginia, through which public high school educators participate in the Virginia College & Career Readiness Initiative, designed to integrate college and career preparedness into high school English courses.

Many of the educators we have worked with over the years have shared insights that we have incorporated into this book. In 2010, we surveyed 50 of these secondary English educators and asked them what language-related challenges are most common in their classrooms. We found four main themes. First, educators wanted to know how to help students understand and use the norms and conventions of standardized English.

- "How can I help students know when and how to use appropriate forms of language in different settings?"
- "My students struggle with writing, particularly with tenses and spelling. Most of them write the way they speak and tend to spell words the way they say them. I have also noticed aspects of online language and the use of abbreviations based on texting in some of my students' writing."
- "My students struggle with adopting a formal tone for written responses and certain audiences."

Second, many educators wanted to develop students' proficiency in standardized English while respecting and valuing students' individual voices and linguistic heritages.

- "Many of my culturally and linguistically diverse students struggle between learning the 'rules' of writing and keeping their own voice. How can I help these students?"
- "My students struggle with different pronunciations, which can also cause spelling challenges. Some students also struggle with the idea of writing and speaking in 'proper' English, mainly because that labels how they already speak as 'improper.'"
- "It seems that in our culture, speaking standard English is almost a prerequisite for success. On the other hand, holding onto linguistic traditions and culture is extremely important. I would like to help my students have both."

Third, educators wanted to learn ways of discussing language, culture, and diversity that would help students understand and respect one another's modes of communication and culture.

- "How can I teach students to be more open-minded about language variation?"
- "How can I help students stop drawing conclusions about their peers based on the way they speak?"
- "I have many students who speak 'standard English' whose main challenge is understanding the idea of language variation, period. They immediately dismiss other dialects as being wrong, and it's hard to convince them otherwise."

Fourth, educators discussed the challenges that can arise when students read and respond to texts that feature language variation.

- "My students struggle initially with authors such as Mark Twain, Zora Neale Hurston, and Flannery O'Connor. The dialogue and narration is in a different dialect than they are used to hearing, which frustrates many students."
- "I teach *To Kill a Mockingbird,* and my students struggle a bit with the dialect of the dialogue, plus there's also the issue of the racial slurs used in the text."
- "I would like some tips and guidelines on how to effectively reach students who not only find literature boring, but who also cannot fully understand the language being used in it."

In *We Do Language*, we address these points. We model how to hold classroom conversations about language, diversity, culture, and representation, and we provide information about language variation that helps students understand and interpret the rich dialogue that appears in texts that are commonly read in the secondary English classroom. We discuss how educators can value students' home languages and language varieties and build on them while teaching students about the norms and conventions of standardized English.

We also explore how educators can value their own language variation and draw on their own linguistic identities as resources in their teaching. Recently, a veteran English educator explained to Anne that she had never thought about the specific role of her own language in the English classes she taught and had never figured out a constructive way to bring up issues of language variation. The educator spoke a nonstandardized variety of English herself, and she had always sought to cover up her variety, rather than to use it as an instrument of learning and as a literary device. Her realization of the importance of discussing and honoring language variation—for her students and for herself—was therefore both personal and professional. Our framework and strategies enable educators to build on their own strengths of linguistic versatility, modeling the skills of flexibility in language that are critical for students to develop, in secondary settings and beyond.

Throughout this book, we explain key concepts and provide teaching ideas that directly transfer to classroom practice. We offer classroom-ready strategies, questions, exercises, and activities that are good points of reflection and that can be used to promote classroom discussion. We share thoughts, perspectives, and insights from educators and students about the significance of language and culture. Some of the educators' vignettes recount personal journeys or moments in understanding language variation, while others report on classroom activities and instructional strategies. While these materials are designed for secondary English educators and students, they can easily be adapted for younger or older students. By providing these resources, we move the conversation from the question of *why* consider language variation to *how* to effectively do so, making linguistic information and language awareness tangible and relevant to the classroom.

WHO WE ARE

Language and culture are deeply personal and deeply rooted. As we explained in our first book, "one's language and culture are not like a set of clothes that can be easily changed" (Charity Hudley & Mallinson, 2011, p. 13). Who we are—our backgrounds, heritages, and upbringings—affect and are affected by language and culture. Language and culture also influence the novels, poems, plays, and other literature that speak to us, from youth to adulthood. In this section, we share our linguistic and literary autobiographies and tell about who we are as individuals and educators. We use this exercise (see Box 1.1 on p. 6), which builds on Labov (1987), in our own classes and workshops to reveal the significance of language, literature, literacy, and culture. By writing and sharing our linguistic and literary autobiographies, we set the stage for others to do the same, an exchange that fosters linguistically and culturally informed communication.

Anne's Linguistic and Literary Autobiography

I grew up in Varina, Virginia, a rural area zoned for agriculture just east of Richmond. Every week as a child I'd stand by my Rural Route mailbox, waiting for my Dr. Seuss and Disney book club books to arrive. Along those

BOX 1.1. CURRICULAR CONNECTIONS: Linguistic and Literary Autobiographies

This exercise guides us to think about the social context of language, literature, culture, and identity. These questions can be used as prompts for written essays or in classroom discussions.

- Where are you from? Where have you lived? Who have you lived with? Which of these social details do you think may have influenced the way you speak now?
- Is there a language you used to know that you don't speak so well anymore? Did you ever pass (even for a short time) as a native speaker of some other language?
- Have you noticed any differences between the way you speak and the way your parents/guardians speak? What did they have to say about your use of language at home? Who was likely to correct your language?
- Do you remember particular comments or instances where your speech was remarked on? Has anyone ever told you to talk in a certain way—or not to talk in a certain way? For example, maybe you have been told to speak "less country," "more formally," or with a higher or lower pitch. How did this feedback affect you?
- Have you ever been praised for your use of standardized English? Are there any grammar conventions that you are good at remembering? Are there any that are harder for you? Do you remember when you were finally able to master a grammar rule (at least some of the time)? How long did it take?
- Have you ever gone to another country and struggled with the language? What types of issues might be faced by people who go to another country and have to learn a new language?
- What literature spoke to you as a child? Can you recall specific nursery rhymes, fairy tales, poems, stories, or songs? What do you remember about the words, rhymes, tone, style, and figurative language they used? Were different languages or language varieties used in any of your favorite childhood literature or music?
- What literature speaks to you now and why? Do you consider yourself a writer, a poet, or a storyteller? In what ways do you engage with literature in everyday settings? What about on holidays or significant occasions? How does literature matter in your personal life compared to your professional life as an educator?

rural roads, I cherished and learned the language varieties found in and around the places where I grew up, and I continue to do so, as the College of William & Mary is just 45 minutes down the road from Varina.

I am from a historically multiracial background (African American, Native American, and White), but in many senses, in Virginia, the one-drop rule still persists, and I am proud to be African American. Our very diverse, very colorful family rings of laughter and song. Early on I gained the skills of quick verbal repartee and grandiose storytelling, and I learned that just as much can be learned outside of school as in school. I cherished the *Value Tales* series by Spencer Johnson and Ann Donegan Johnson. I also have always loved to read the dictionary and reference books. I treasured my sets of *Encyclopedia Britannica*, both the grown-ups' brown and the children's red versions. I attended a predominantly White prep school, where I searched for writing that reflected my story, particularly biographies and autobiographies of African American leaders, including Harriet Tubman, Martin Luther King Jr., Marian Anderson, and Ralph Bunche. I also loved Mildred Taylor's *Roll of Thunder, Hear My Cry*, Louise Fitzhugh's *Nobody's Family Is Going to Change*, and Toni Morrison's *Sula*.

My family has always been very important to me, and my grandmothers were strong role models. My paternal grandmother (my Nana) was raised working class in a farming community, and although she was a top student at the Virginia Randolph School, segregation and financial resources limited her educational options, and she was not able to go to college. Nevertheless, my Nana made the best of what she had, even practicing with me the French vocabulary that she remembered from high school. She was a natural pianist and singer and could command a church with her rendition of "What a Friend We Have in Jesus." My paternal grandfather (my Papa) read multiple newspapers a day and kept me informed about what was going on in our communities and in the world. In contrast, my maternal grandmother (my Grandma) held master's degrees in English and history; her master's thesis addressed the need for more libraries in rural African American areas in the U.S. South. She taught me to read by age 3 and had me reciting poetry and conversing on topics in African American history by age 8. I retain her love of poetry to this day and carried her copies of the poetry of Gwendolyn Brooks and Milton's *Paradise Lost* with me to college. She introduced me to what is still my favorite poetry book: Dudley Randall's *The Black Poets*.

After graduating from high school, I left Virginia to attend Harvard. After about a year I picked up some of the features of a New England accent and even learned the lilt of Seamus Heaney as he read from his work in Helen Vendler's "Poems, Poets, Poetry" class. Graduate school in Philadelphia also brought a more intimate knowledge of language as it is spoken in the inner cities of the Northeast; I read the language in Elijah Anderson's *Code of the Street*, and I found my love for sociological ethnography. After my studies were over and I returned to Virginia, I quickly readopted the linguistic markers that are characteristic of my native variety of English—the variety that is steeped in the Southern Oral History tradition and rich with the songs sung in the wayside churches of the South.

I am now associate professor at the College of William & Mary in Williamsburg, Virginia, where I am affiliated with the School of Education and the departments of English, linguistics, Africana studies, community studies, and women's studies. I am also the director of the Linguistics Laboratory and am the inaugural William & Mary Professor of Community Studies. I direct the William & Mary Scholars Program and codirect the William & Mary Scholars Undergraduate Research Experience (WMSURE). My role as director of WMSURE is to build a program for students that will serve as a national model for nurturing the academic potential of high achieving students from diverse backgrounds. The poetry of Nikki Giovanni and Alice Walker guide me on that journey.

As my career has progressed, I have seen the direct need to engage secondary and postsecondary English educators together in conversation. To this end, I have been a lead researcher on the Virginia Capstone English Project, the Senior English Seminar Academy, and the College & Career Readiness Initiative, statewide projects funded by the State Council of Higher Education for Virginia to align secondary and postsecondary English education goals. I also work with secondary English education students and doctoral students at the College of William & Mary on many of the same topics and themes that are covered in this book. The story we are now writing is our own.

Christine's Linguistic and Literary Autobiography

I grew up in a White, middle-class family outside the small town of Salisbury, North Carolina. From preschool onward, my days were filled with the rich sounds of the language of the Piedmont region of North Carolina. As I recited jump rope rhymes on the playground and learned the rhymes and rhythms of hand clapping games like "Miss Mary Mack," I developed an accent that was never strong but was unmistakably Southern. At home, I heard different languages and language varieties. My parents, who were originally from New York and Pennsylvania, moved to North Carolina for college in the early 1970s. They found the South to be a warm and hospitable place and never left, and over time they picked up some Southern language patterns, words, and phrases, including *y'all* and *hey*. Although I didn't know my grandparents on my father's side, my paternal great-grandmother was a high school teacher who attended Syracuse University's Teacher's College in the early 1900s. My maternal grandparents came from Germany; they met and married in New York City and later moved to North Carolina. They spoke a mixture of English and German, which my brother and I heard from the time we were born. We sang German songs with my grandmother, and I recited nursery rhymes such as "Ringel, Ringel, Reihe" alongside the English version, "Ring around the Rosy."

As a child, some of my earliest memories of language came from songs. I loved to sing along with everything from ballads such as "Oh! Susanna" and "Oh My Darling, Clementine" to church hymns, Christmas carols, and the music of Neil Diamond, James Taylor, and Simon and Garfunkel. I learned to read at age 2—the first phrase I read out loud was *thank you*, and the first word I remember sounding out on my own was *begun*. Once I started reading, I didn't stop. I read the books of Dr. Seuss, the tales of Beatrix Potter, the tales of Winnie-the-Pooh and children's poems by A. A. Milne, and fairy tales from around the world. I loved books with strong heroines, such as *Pippi Longstocking*, *Anne of Green Gables*, *Little Women*, and the *Nancy Drew* series, and delighted in the extraordinary language in the books of Roald Dahl. As I got older I branched out to other works by women authors, such as the poetry of Emily Dickinson and the novels of Charlotte Brontë, Kate Chopin, and Amy Tan.

In high school, I started to explore Southern literature, reading William Faulkner, Toni Morrison, Zora Neale Hurston, and Flannery O'Connor. Comparing the themes and voices in these novels to those in *Gone with the Wind*, *Uncle Tom's Cabin*, and *To Kill a Mockingbird*, I became aware of the deep complexities of language and culture in the South and of the ways that authors strive to represent in literature the sounds of language spoken with a Southern cadence. I went to college at the University of North Carolina and graduate school at North Carolina State University, where my favorite classes in sociology, linguistics, and English dealt with the importance of language to people's identities, both as individuals and as members of cultural and social groups. At both of these Southern universities, I delved into my study of language and culture in the South and Appalachia, balancing my reading of articles from academic journals with the novels of Lee Smith and the poetry of A. R. Ammons.

I now live in Baltimore, a city that has been called the northernmost Southern town and the southernmost Northern town. Here, residents say *y'all* as well as *hon*, get *carry out* (not *takeout*), and eat *snowballs* (*snow cones*). I have learned about Baltimore's many ethnic groups and neighborhoods, rich cultural history of artists and musicians, and strong literary tradition that includes Edgar Allan Poe and Frederick Douglass. My husband and I are introducing our daughter to the sights and sounds of this city that she will call home. As we expose her to our combined library of diverse texts, oral and written, that have spoken to us in our lives, we are watching her develop her own love of language and literature.

In the courses that I teach as associate professor at the University of Maryland–Baltimore County (UMBC), I guide students to connect their own backgrounds, cultures, educational experiences, and language and literacy traditions with the texts that are read and produced in educational settings. My students engage in interdisciplinary study, drawing connections among language, literacy, and culture, and they conduct their own research on topics that have real-world implications, such as how to foster the success of culturally and linguistically diverse students and promote social and educational change.

Across the United States, in our schools and communities, children and adults like me, my daughter, husband, brother, parents, grandparents, and students have multilingual and multicultural stories to tell. I believe we must understand our cultural backgrounds to be able to teach and learn from each other, and language is a key piece of the puzzle. As we welcome and integrate each other's linguistic and cultural perspectives, we lift up our students, our schools, our communities, and ourselves.

OUR GOALS FOR THIS BOOK

In reading this book, we hope that you will ponder your own personal perspectives, linguistic heritages, and cultural backgrounds, finding points of similarity as well as difference between our experiences and your own. This journey of discovery is an important one for students, too. As they come to know who they are and how they communicate, they are better equipped to understand their own linguistic styles and those of others, to respect and engage with similarities and differences, and to analyze texts by authors with diverse voices and standpoints.

In Chapter 1, we have introduced our rationale for exploring how we "do language," in our everyday lives and in secondary English classrooms, where language, literature, literacy, culture, and identity intersect.

In Chapter 2, "Language Varies," we take a closer look at the nuances of language, language variation, and communication by introducing three linguistic truths. These truths are central to helping students develop their linguistic awareness and a deeper understanding of language and communication.

In Chapter 3, "Language and Culture: Having Courageous Conversations," we consider how language is intertwined with elements of classroom culture and expectations for students. We discuss the concepts of culture and of cultural and linguistic capital. We also explore linguistic and cultural challenges in the form of communication breakdowns, stereotypes and prejudices, microaggressions, ethnic labels and slurs, and bullying. We close by examining linguistic agency, and we discuss how culturally and linguistically responsive education can foster communication across lines of difference.

In Chapter 4, "Language Variation in Literature," we apply a sociolinguistic lens to examine literature commonly taught in secondary English classrooms that reflects rich language variation. We examine how the use of language variation can allow authors and readers to express identities and to have important and sometimes challenging cultural conversations. We also highlight how the use of linguistically diverse literature can help engage all students in the secondary English curriculum.

In Chapter 5, "Doing Language: The Transition to College and Beyond," we focus on how educators can help their students develop the communication skills they need in order to meet the complex and varied linguistic expectations of the college environment and to add their voice and perspective to academic discourse. By encouraging students to investigate the role of language in their lives and in the world, educators can guide students to tell their own stories. In so doing, students also become successful speakers and writers who possess strong oral and written skills as well as other "21st-century skills" that are integral to success in college and beyond.

On our website, www.charityhudleymallinson.com/wdl, we provide additional information about language, literature, and secondary English education, including sources for further reading, podcasts, videos, and other multimedia content, so that educators and students can learn more about the rich sounds and structures of English and its many varieties in talk and in texts.

CHAPTER 2

Language Varies

Many of us are aware of language differences and the linguistic choices available to us as speakers of English, especially when we encounter words we didn't grow up hearing ourselves. We often notice whether someone says *soda* or *pop*, for instance—a question asked on the website, www.popvssoda.com. Do we say *shopping cart* or *buggy*? How do we pronounce *dog*, and what about *coffee*? How do we feel about *isn't* versus *ain't*, *hanged* versus *hung*, and *sneaked* versus *snuck*? The ways we use English can vary across groups, within groups, and even by speaker (Wolfram & Schilling-Estes, 2006). Diversity in language does not only apply to people who speak different languages; there is also diversity within languages, including English in the United States, which is the focus of this book.

Where does language diversity come from and how can we best understand it? This chapter addresses the key question: How do we value students' home varieties and build on them while learning standardized English? To answer this question, we present three linguistic truths, and we examine language variation in ways that help educators determine how best to approach the language arts standards that are often set forth in their classrooms and schools. Discussion boxes, exercises and activities, and quotes and vignettes from educators throughout this chapter help model how to approach the complexity and variation of the English language in secondary English curricula.

LINGUISTIC TRUTH #1: COMMUNICATION OCCURS IN SOCIAL CONTEXTS

Communication occurs in social contexts (Labov, 1972b). When we communicate, we do so in ways that are influenced by many factors, including historical and social context, the communities we live in, the institutions and social organizations we participate in, and the backgrounds, cultures, and identities of ourselves and others. Communication is a complex and nuanced behavior; it is both innate and learned. Being a good communicator depends on using language in acceptable, appropriate, and effective ways.

The linguist, anthropologist, and folklorist Dell Hymes (1966) coined the term *communicative competence*. People who are communicatively competent are able to accomplish tasks with language, express and interpret intentions, and understand the different social and linguistic functions that language can serve.

Current educational standards recognize that students must be able to understand and navigate different types of English. For example, according to the Common Core English Language Arts Standards (Common Core State Standards Initiative, 2012a), Students must "[d]emonstrate command of the conventions of standard English grammar and usage when writing or speaking." To paraphrase, this aim seeks to help students become *communicatively competent* in multiple varieties of English. "Key Points in English Language Arts" from the Common Core State Standards are included in Box 2.1 on p. 14 along with discussion questions for educators to consider.

The National Council of Teachers of English and the International Reading Association (1996) have similarly advocated that students learn to communicate effectively in the "language of wider communication" and to "engage in discussions of when and where this language of wider communication can and should be used." Through this process, students "further their knowledge of audience, purpose, and context, and in so doing discover something of the social significance of different language practices" (p. 34). These organizations also emphasized the importance of building an educational climate that fosters an understanding of and respect for linguistic and cultural variation (p. 42). According to these guidelines, successful students are aware of and respect language diversity, and they are able to make informed choices about how to use language in different communicative situations.

Register

Among humans, patterns of communication are generally organized into languages. Sometimes, people may use the same language yet still misunderstand each other. While some forms of communication are perfectly shared, others are variable. Some aspects of communication, such as a smile, seem to be universal. Of course, the question of when it is appropriate to smile is far from universal (Biber & Finegan, 1994).

The term *register* refers to the different ways that language is used in different social situations and contexts. Most of us communicate differently with family members compared to friends, acquaintances, and strangers, whether we are talking, writing, texting, blogging, and so on. We often

BOX 2.1. CURRICULAR CONNECTIONS: Key Points in English Language Arts

The following "Key Points in English Language Arts" for Speaking and Listening and Language directly address communication as set by the Common Core State Standards (Common Core State Standards Initiative, 2012b). Some important questions for educators to consider in relation to these key points are: How can educators best prepare students to be communicatively competent? What teaching strategies are commonly used and how might they vary? In what ways are students in your classroom or school successful in meeting these standards? What challenges might they face? How might these challenges be addressed?

Speaking and Listening

"The standards require that students gain, evaluate, and present increasingly complex information, ideas, and evidence through listening and speaking as well as through media."

"An important focus of the speaking and listening standards is academic discussion in one-on-one, small-group, and whole-class settings. Formal presentations are one important way such talk occurs, but so is the more informal discussion that takes place as students collaborate to answer questions, build understanding, and solve problems."

Language

"The standards expect that students will grow their vocabularies through a mix of conversations, direct instruction, and reading. The standards will help students determine word meanings, appreciate the nuances of words, and steadily expand their repertoire of words and phrases."

"The standards help prepare students for real life experience at college and in 21st century careers. The standards recognize that students must be able to use formal English in their writing and speaking but that they must also be able to make informed, skillful choices among the many ways to express themselves through language."

also use language differently in our numerous social roles—as an educator, spouse, mother, daughter, sibling, churchgoer, or sports team member, for example. For many students, learning appropriate ways of communicating in school has much to do with register selection. Language used inside the classroom is different from language used on the playground, just as the way a student is expected to talk to a principal often differs from ways of talking to other students (Eckert, 1989). Every school subject also has its own terminology; for instance, the language of a science report is different from a word problem in math or an essay about a novel. Students are expected to communicate in multiple registers, and they are often expected to address educators in school-specific ways. In some schools, educators and

BOX 2.2. FOR LINGUISTIC REFLECTION:
Honorifics

Honorifics are words or phrases used to address or refer to other people; they generally convey esteem or respect. Common honorifics in English are *Ms., Miss, Mrs., Mr., Dr., Ma'am, Sir,* and *Professor.* Opinions on the use of honorifics often vary widely. The following questions can be used as discussion starters.

- Do you teach your students about the use of honorifics? Why or why not? If so, how?
- What honorifics are used when teachers, students, and principals call each other by name? How do you feel about students calling an educator or principal by her or his first name? What about calling an educator or principal by last name only, as in "Hey, Jones"? How about "Yes, ma'am" or "Yes, sir"?
- How do students and educators in your school address each other? Have you ever been in a situation where there was a miscommunication over a student's or educator's use (or lack of use) of a particular honorific?
- Should every school ask students to use the same honorifics? Should it be left up to individual schools or educators to decide which ones to use?
- Should educators use honorifics when talking to their students? Compare and contrast your answers with those of other educators and students.

students call each other by their first names. In others, the use of honorifics, such as *Miss Nancy*, *Mrs. Jones*, or *Dr. B.*, is appropriate. Sometimes, it will be clear to students and educators how these norms are established and how they are communicated within classrooms and schools; at other times, these linguistic and educational expectations may not be apparent.

Certain registers are often seen as being more polite or more socially acceptable than others. In the history of English, words that were borrowed from French were seen as having more prestige, due to the prevailing view that Norman French culture was more refined than the native English culture (Crystal, 2003). Because of this historical and political context, many English words that derive from French are still seen today as being more formal than their Anglo-Saxon counterparts; for example, words such as *perspire*, *dine*, and *commence* are seen as being more refined than *sweat*, *eat*, and *begin*.

Students are often not aware of the finer nuances of register, however, and they may use words and phrases that seem too informal for school, even though those words and phrases might be perfectly acceptable in other communicative situations (Biber & Finegan, 1994). By teaching about register, educators can help students attune their ears to language variation. One way to teach secondary English students about register is to guide them to focus on the specifics of communicative situations. The "SPEAKING" model (Hymes, 1974) illustrates the components of communication. SPEAKING is a mnemonic device, in which each letter stands for a different component. As we discuss each element of the model, we apply it to the example of an end-of-the-school-year awards ceremony.

S: *Setting* and *scene* stand for the time, place, and psychological characteristics of communication. For example, in the setting of an end-of-the-school-year awards ceremony, the scene might be formal and celebratory.

P: *Participants* refer to speakers and audience—intended and unintended. At the awards ceremony, the principal might give a speech. The intended audience is the auditorium of educators, parents, and students, but there may be an unintended audience, such as the custodial staff members who also hear the speech.

E: *Ends* stands for the purpose of the communication and what participants seek to accomplish. The purpose or goal of the principal's speech might be to welcome the audience to the ceremony.

A: *Act sequence* refers to the form and the order of the communicative event—what is said and how. The principal's welcome speech might begin as a response to an educator who introduces the principal. Perhaps the audience applauds the educator and the principal, and then a student gives the main address.

K: *Key* represents the tone, manner, or spirit of the communicative event (similar to the way music is written in a certain key). The key can be conveyed verbally and nonverbally and may change during communication. Perhaps the presentation of awards begins in a serious tone when the formal awards are given and becomes more lighthearted when fun awards are presented.

I: *Instrumentalities* stand for the forms and styles of speech that are used and how speakers are strategic in their rhetoric—that is, how speakers select one register or another to convey a specific message. Perhaps the educator's introduction is given in a register that uses standardized English features in order to signal formality, whereas the principal's speech is given in a register that uses nonstandardized English features in order to signal approachability.

N: *Norms* refer to the social conventions governing the communication, including the participants' actions and how the event unfolds. For example, social norms generally dictate that a principal's speech should not be interrupted.

G: *Genre* refers to the type of communication. The principal's communication takes place in the genre of giving a speech. Lectures, poems, letters, toasts, and stories are other examples of genres, which can be oral or written.

The SPEAKING model can be used in the secondary English classroom to help students understand how to shift their own styles of communication and how to interpret others' styles and shifts, in spoken and written form. Once students identify the social components of a communicative situation, it is easier to figure out which other grammatical and stylistic conventions to follow. For example, if students are asked to prepare a speech to give to the class, it may be useful to have them identify the *genre* (speech), the *key* (formal), and the *participants* (teacher and classmates). The model can also be compared and contrasted with other models of rhetoric that students learn in secondary English classrooms, such as Aristotle's model of logos, ethos, and pathos (Freese, 1924; see also Lunsford, Ruszkiewicz, & Walters, 2012). In Box 2.3 on p. 18, a 4th-grade language arts/writing educator described how she helped her students understand the *participants* component of the SPEAKING model through an exercise in which they adapted their roles as speakers to two different classroom audiences.

When teaching students how to adapt their speaking and writing to different situations, it is important to remember that not all language differences can be explained with the concept of register alone. Varieties of English are often characterized as "informal," but this assessment is based on a misunderstanding of the difference between *language variety* and *register*. Whereas *register* refers to differences in language use according to social situation (often along dimensions of formality and informality), a *variety* is the cluster of language forms, features, and patterns that are used by different social groups. For example, consider the variety of English that is often called African American English (discussed in depth in Charity Hudley & Mallinson, 2011). It is not the case that this variety of English is always informal. African Americans regularly use African American English in many formal situations: during political speeches, in church, and at funerals, to name a few. Listening to speeches by orators such as Martin Luther King Jr. quickly reveals how African American rhetorical style can be employed to great effect, including in formal situations. In sum, the term *language variety* focuses our attention on how a language varies, by factors such as region of origin, gender, social class, age, race/ethnicity, culture, and personal[ity,] but it usually does not refer to aspects of style or formality/informali[ty;] those considerations generally belong to discussions of *register*.

All individuals, whether using a standardized or a nonstandardi[zed va-]riety of English, adjust their language to suit different social situat[ions.]

BOX 2.3. AN EDUCATOR'S VIGNETTE: An Exercise on Audience Design

Jessica Medina, 4th-Grade Language Arts/Writing Teacher

As part of a final project for a seminar in sociolinguistics that I took as a master's student in a Curriculum and Instruction program, I developed this idea for a project to help teach students about audience. Then, I used this activity with my students in my writing class.

I began by asking the students to tell a story to their friends. The topic was school uniforms and how they felt about them. The students were speaking very passionately and openly, not worrying about their peers and their reactions.

The next day, I had lined up parent volunteers to come to my classroom and play the role of "president," "principal," etc. I asked my students to retell their stories and opinions to the parent volunteers. The students all style-shifted on their own.

Afterward, we debriefed as a class and talked about how the students had changed their language and their body language, depending on the different audiences and settings. Our conversation helped my students become aware of their linguistic behaviors, which would have otherwise gone unnoticed. Finally, I asked my students to write about this experience in their journals, where they were able to explore their reactions to how they, their peers, and the parent volunteers used language.

this ability is learned over time. Many adults are adept at being able to use different registers, whereas students often must be taught explicitly how to do so. To build the skill of register selection, educators may ask students to describe, record, analyze, and interpret how their language is the same or different when they do a range of activities, including giving a class presentation or report, arguing, talking on the phone, greeting friends, greeting family members, and greeting educators (Goodman, 2003). What may seem like disrespect, inappropriate tone, or informal delivery in writing and speaking may occur when students do not understand which register is implicitly expected of them in the classroom; therefore, it is important to teach the nuances of register selection.

Attention to register can particularly benefit struggling students (Fisher & Frey, 2011). One educator who worked with us explained an exercise that she created and used in her high school English class that had the following guidelines: "Compose a short skit or conversation written entirely in the daily language you use outside of school with family and friends—for example, a dialogue between a mother and her son, or a short skit about a group of friends deciding what to do on Saturday night. Be creative!" The teacher explained that, after they finished the exercise, one of her students—

who until this point had refused to engage with her on issues of writing—let her sit with him and talk about English usage. She recalled, "We looked for instances where he had written *suppose to* instead of *supposed to* throughout his essay, and he was open to talking about his use of language and also about tone and register. Just by opening that door, we were able to have the conversation about what everyday language can convey versus what standardized English can convey." Creative exercises such as this skit can help secondary English students learn to navigate between their everyday language and the norms and conventions of standardized English.

Is There a Standard English?

Thus far, we have discussed that language is adapted according to different social situations. Often, the concept of language flexibility and diversity

BOX 2.4. AN EDUCATOR'S VIGNETTE: Teaching About Register

April Lawrence, Doctoral Student in Education at the College of William & Mary and Former Secondary English Educator

What happens when a working-class Southern girl becomes a high school English teacher? Identity crisis. I realized pretty early on in my college experience that the language of academia was more formal and much less colorful than the diction, tone, and voice I had grown up hearing. There was no *Well, I suwannee!* in college English, nor were there any *might coulds.*

When I stood in front of my first high school classroom—32 11th-graders in a culturally diverse school district—I realized that they might feel the same sort of identity crisis that I had experienced in academia. So, I put it out there on the table for them: "You know what, y'all? I don't speak like this all the time. Do you think I say things like, 'That was a great point; could you support it with some evidence?' when I'm hanging out with my friends? Heck no! And the way that I speak around my friends is slightly different from the way I speak around my Grandma. Do you think I say to Grandma, 'What the—no, he did not! Oh. My. God.' Of course not!"

As you might imagine, this honest discussion opened the door to numerous teachable moments and classroom instructional opportunities for exploring tone, voice, diction, audience, register, purpose, and persuasive techniques. Recognizing out loud that language variation is inextricably linked to identity and encouraging class discussion about situational shifts in language helped me to get buy-in from many students who had felt that they just "weren't very good at English." I highly recommend facilitating these types of conversations with your students, listening to their voices, and making those voices a part of your instruction . . . *y'all.*

brings up questions about whether there is a standard English. Most people have strong opinions about what types of grammar, speech, reading, and writing are "standard" or "proper" (Lippi-Green, 2011). The term *standard English* is commonly used to refer to a preferred style of English (for example, this term is used in the Common Core State Standards for English Language Arts). Other terms include *formal English*, *proper English*, *educated English*, *good English*, and *correct English*.

When we consider these terms in light of our linguistic truths, many difficulties and complexities arise. The term *standard English* may suggest that some sort of single standard variety of English exists, irrespective of social norms, registers, or situational context. Because language is a social behavior, how people communicate is always situated within specific contexts and interactions. Different situations yield different forms of talk, and ideas of what counts as "correct" or "standard" change over time. After all, no one today still speaks what was considered "correct English" in Chaucer's time, nor do we in the United States use what might be considered the proper "Queen's English" in Great Britain.

There is no single agreed-upon and canonized standard variety of English. Grammar book–style English is often viewed as the target for how students should express themselves in school settings and how adults should express themselves in professional settings. But in fact, grammar books, dictionaries, and pundits who debate what is "proper" rarely agree (Curzan, 2000). Sources that purport to be standard English authorities sometimes use inconsistent, misleading, or vague terminology as well as *you know it when you see it* definitions that can make teaching and learning about English unnecessarily difficult and confusing (Charity Hudley & Mallinson, 2011).

Throughout this book (and in our first book), we have avoided the use of the term *standard English*, because it implies homogeneity and oversimplifies linguistic realities. Instead, we use the slightly different term *standardized English*. This term, which we and other scholars use (Dunn & Lindblom, 2003; Richardson, 2003a), makes the parallel that just as specific types of knowledge are valued on standardized tests, so, too, are specific types of language valued within the educational system. It also reflects the fact that powerful people and institutions, including the media, are involved in decisions about when and how to endorse one variety of English over others. Political, social, and cultural privilege has often determined which language varieties of English were deemed to be more prestigious, socially acceptable, or "standard" than others (Bonfiglio, 2002; Bourdieu, 1991). As Romaine (1994, p. 84) noted, standardization is not an inherent characteristic of language but an "acquired or deliberately and artificially imposed characteristic." In other words, if any language, language variety, or linguistic feature is considered prestigious, it is only because that type of language is spoken or valued by socially, economically, and politically powerful people and is not due to any independent or inherent linguistic qualities (Lippi-Green, 2011).

At the same time, throughout this book we include many quotes and perspectives from others, including secondary English educators, who sometimes use different terminology than we do. They may use the term *dialect* where we use *language variety*, or they may use *standard English* where we use *standardized English*. Although we explain why we use specific terms, we do not view ourselves as guardians of terminology. Instead, in keeping with our model of linguistic diversity, we respect the terms used by others and allow for a plurality of linguistic choices.

LINGUISTIC TRUTH #2: LANGUAGE IS ALWAYS CHANGING

Language is always changing, to different degrees and for different reasons. Each generation creates new words, new pronunciations, and new ways of phrasing thoughts and ideas. Language also changes when different cultures come into contact, borrowing and lending each other's modes of communication. English itself has been formed and transformed by contact with other languages, and in turn English has influenced other languages around the world (Crystal, 2012). As new elements are incorporated into any language over time, outmoded grammatical constructions, pronunciations, spellings, words, and styles fall out of favor and eventually are replaced. Even school-specific vocabulary sees a great deal of variation and change. Terminology such as "briefly constructed responses," "power writing," and "21st-century learning" often varies from school setting to school setting and may or may not stay in vogue.

Most students come to school with at least the general awareness that language varies and that different situations can call for different types of language to be used. For example, Higgs, Manning, and Miller (1995) found that Appalachian children, by 2nd or 3rd grade, had already picked up on differences between language patterns used at home versus school. Educators can build on students' perceptions about language and develop them by encouraging students to analyze the differences they see and hear, perhaps in the language patterns of parents compared to children or educators compared to students. More advanced students can analyze historical changes in the English language, whether by studying texts from different time periods or by studying how dictionaries have changed over generations. English is generally described as having five distinct periods—Pre- or Proto-English, Old English, Middle English, Early Modern, and Modern

English (Crystal, 2003), and Box 2.5 provides examples of literary texts from these eras. By comparing and contrasting linguistic features across these texts, students can consider how English has changed and is currently changing, in ways that may be ephemeral or permanent. Guiding students to think about language change can increase their linguistic awareness, which can help them develop their communicative competence.

BOX 2.5. CURRICULAR CONNECTIONS:
From Old English to Modern English in Literature

This exercise investigates language change in English. In the passages below, what similarities and differences exist in vocabulary, spelling, grammar, punctuation, and other elements? Changes in pronunciation can also reveal how English has evolved. Our website, www.charityhudleymallinson.com/wdl, provides links where passages from these poems are read out loud. Educators and students can consider questions such as: What pronunciation changes are heard across these passages? What pronunciation changes are occurring in English today? Which of them seem more fleeting and which might persist?

Old English

Excerpt from Beowulf *(c. 900 CE)*

oft Scyld Scefing sceaþena þreatum,
monegum mægþum, meodosetla ofteah,
egsode eorlas, syððanærest wearð
feasceaft funden; he þæs frofre gebad,
weox under wolcnum, weorðmyndum þah,
oð þæt him æghwylc ymbsittendra
ofer hronrade hyran scolde,
gomban gyldan; þæt wæs god cyning!

Middle English

Excerpt from The Canterbury Tales *(Chaucer, c. 1343–1400)*

Whan that April with his showres soote
The droughte of March hath perced to the roote,
And bathed every veine in swich licour,
Of which vertu engendred is the flowr;
Whan Zephyrus eek with his sweete breeth
Inspired hath in every holt and heeth
The tendre croppes, and the yonge sonne
Hath in the Ram his halve cours yronne,
And smale fowles maken melodye

That sleepen al the night with open yë—
So priketh hem Nature in hir corages—
Thanne longen folk to goon on pilgrimages . . .

Early Modern English

Excerpt from "Death Be Not Proud" (Donne, 1633)

Death, be not proud, though some have called thee
Mighty and dreadful, for thou art not so;
For those whom thou think'st thou dost overthrow,
Die not, poor Death, nor yet canst thou kill me.
From rest and sleep, which but thy pictures be,
Much pleasure; then from thee much more must flow,
And soonest our best men with thee do go,
Rest of their bones, and soul's delivery.

Modern English

Excerpt from "since feeling is first" (Cummings, 1924)

my blood approves,
and kisses are a better fate
than wisdom
lady i swear by all flowers. Don't cry
—the best gesture of my brain is less than
your eyelids' flutter which says

we are for each other: then
laugh, leaning back in my arms
for life's not a paragraph

And death i think is no parenthesis

The Language of Shakespeare

Any discussion of English language and literature would not be complete without mentioning William Shakespeare. Shakespeare is a fixture of secondary English curricula, and his work provides insight into our second linguistic truth: language varies and is always changing.

Shakespeare altered the English language in permanent ways (Macrone, 1990), and his creative use of language illustrates the beauty and genius in finding new modes of expression. Students can study the many words and phrases coined by Shakespeare that contemporary English speakers continue to use every day—from *eyeball*, *assassination*, and *shooting star* to *mind's eye*, *love is blind*, and *all that glitters is not gold*—and trace the relatively recent history of these words and phrases in the evolution of English. Students can also consider modern-day correlates to Shakespeare: What contemporary figures are coining new words, phrases, grammatical constructions, and pronunciations? How are linguistic innovations picked up and spread within groups or throughout society today?

The works of Shakespeare can also be used to discuss both the value of linguistic conventions and the value in occasionally departing from them. In his sonnets, Shakespeare typically follows the conventions of the sonnet genre, but the fact that these conventions exist also allows him occasionally to deviate from them, often for effect or emphasis. Just as Shakespearean sonnets are expected to follow specific conventions, students today have specific conventions they are expected to follow, such as when writing a school essay, a personal statement, or an email to a teacher. Other conventions operate when students write texts to friends, casual emails, tweets, blog posts, and instant messages, although these conventions are not generally codified. Students can therefore explore the linguistic conventions that Shakespeare worked with and compare them to those that they encounter: Like Shakespeare, students today must make choices, in everyday and in academic settings. Through these sorts of exercises, students can build a stronger understanding of how speakers and writers engage with linguistic conventions and routinely shift their use of language, along stylistic lines and within different genres, to meet their communicative purposes.

In addition, when studying Shakespeare's plays, students can be guided to examine how language variation is used and portrayed (Blank, 1996). Shakespeare included many characters who represent speakers from the lower classes, from ethnic and gender minority groups, and from England's diverse regions, and through them he illustrated important social, cultural, and regional differences of his time. In *Henry V*, soldiers from the four corners of the British Isles are brought together to invade France, and this regional diversity is mirrored in the language of the characters of the Englishman, Irishman, Welshman, and Scot. When reflecting differences in social class, Shakespeare not only wrote in the dialogue of the upper class and royalty, but also in dialogue that represented the speech of those who were not part of the gentry. Due to the architecture of the theaters in which Shakespeare's plays were performed and the economics of putting on a play in Elizabethan England, plays needed to appeal to multiple audiences. They not only had to capture the interest of the aristocrats, who sat in the balconies, but also that of the "groundlings" who paid a penny for entrance and who stood around the stage. As a result, Shakespeare's plays are rich in linguistic diversity, often highlighting language varieties that were very different from the Queen's English, the privileged variety at the time (Blank, 1996).

In fact, Shakespeare often upheld characters who represent groups that were stigmatized in Elizabethan times and provided them with powerful language to express themselves. In *Othello*, although people who looked like the Moorish prince from North Africa would have faced much prejudice in Elizabethan society, Shakespeare had Othello speak commandingly, in the language of the aristocracy. In *The Merchant of Venice*, Shylock's speech pleading his humanity and moral equality makes a case for the equal worth of Jews, who were at the time a highly stigmatized group. Shakespeare also allowed his female characters to share linguistic equality with (and frequently have linguistic superiority over) their male counterparts. In *The Merchant of Venice*, Portia dons men's clothes to argue as a lawyer, illustrating through her words that she is just as good as a man. In *Much Ado About Nothing*, Beatrice is more than the linguistic match of Benedict. In *Othello*, Desdemona is assured and self-confident, in general and in high-stakes circumstances, such as speaking in front of the ruling Senate. Her use of language strongly contrasts with prevailing social expectations that equated women's eloquence with their silence (Magnusson, 2004). Shakespeare also often had his characters use language to level distinctions based on social class and education. In *King Lear*, it is the Fool (the court jester) who is the king's wisest advisor and who, through humor and sharp wit, tries to communicate his insight to a stubborn and shortsighted King Lear.

Although he wrote 400 years ago, Shakespeare illustrates the basic linguistic truths that are the cornerstone of our book. Language is a social product, which we use to communicate and express ourselves as social beings. As a natural course of action, language is always changing, frequently for the better. Finally, and perhaps most important, diverse voices are not a deficiency of our society. Rather, they are an asset, enriching our language, enhancing our thinking, and expanding ways to understand our culture and world.

Though Shakespeare has much to offer and is beloved by many, his work is also linguistically complex. Some educators find it challenging to teach Shakespeare, and students may find it difficult to read and understand (hence the popularity of SparkNotes' [2013] *No Fear Shakespeare*, which provides translations of Shakespeare's plays into contemporary English). When we surveyed secondary English educators and asked them to provide an example of a text that their students often struggle with, they overwhelmingly gave responses such as "Shakespearean sonnets," "Shakespearean plays, because they have language that students find perplexing," and "anything by Shakespeare." As one educator put it, "My students struggle with almost every piece of British literature, but Shakespeare is particularly feared and dreaded. However, many eventually find that they like it."

BOX 2.6. AN EDUCATOR'S VIGNETTE: Language in the Works of Shakespeare

Blake Williams,
High School Writing Tutor

The fact that Shakespeare is thought to have coined so many words and phrases that persist in English today allows me to talk to my students about how English is always changing. Just as Shakespeare made English richer, I talk to my students about current linguistic developments. We examine whether texting, hip-hop vocabulary, slang terms, and dialect features are lesser forms of English, as many people claim, or whether (as many of my students and I believe) they can allow us to express ourselves in innovative ways or say the same thing more efficiently.

I also use the fact that Shakespearean English is so different from modern English as a way to practice linguistic flexibility. All of my students have to reach beyond their comfort zones to understand Shakespeare, and as a result each of them goes through the experience of learning a linguistic style that they are not natively familiar with. My students are often faced with multiple language styles in their own worlds, and Shakespeare gives them crucial practice in seeking to understand the beauty of a language style different from their own.

Another high school English educator who worked with us explained that her Southern English-speaking students often use nonstandardized pronunciations that affect how they view prose and verse. For example, one of her students told her, "The word *ball* has two syllables, Ms. Smith, *bah* and *ull.*" As a result, she said, "When I have them write a Shakespearean sonnet, they struggle." Linguistically diverse students who come to school with knowledge of different rhyme patterns may have correspondingly less familiarity with standardized English rhyme patterns, and they may need extra instruction about other rhyme schemes, including those in standardized English (Charity Hudley & Mallinson, 2011). In addition, Shakespeare frequently uses different syllables and rhymes than are used in standardized English today—as in the use of *'fore* for *before* in Sonnet 7, or the rhyming of *again* with *stain* in Sonnet 109—which may require explanation for students to understand.

In the secondary English classroom, students benefit from exploring rhyming conventions in Shakespearean English, contemporary standardized English, and the varieties they speak. They can write two versions of the same sonnet, one that follows the conventions of standardized English and the other that follows those of their home variety, and then compare and contrast the versions in terms of content, form, and function. Students can also compose their own poetry, which can develop their knowledge of and promote their sensitivity to a range of conventions of rhyme, syllables, and word formation (Goodman, 2003). By cultivating their personal voices in writing—what Romano (1995) called "the heart" of literacy (p. xi), students enhance their capacities for linguistic versatility and linguistic awareness.

What About Texting Language?

In thinking about language change, it may be impossible to underestimate the influence of technology on the way today's students communicate. All students write daily, as any educator who has seen students send text after text knows firsthand. The Pew Internet and American Life Project studied the texting habits of young adults in the United States, aged 18 to 29. They found that 97% of young adults who own a cell phone send or receive texts daily. Within this group, "the median 18-24 year old texter sends or receives 50 texts per day (or around 1,500 messages per month)" (Smith, 2011). In the United States, 73% of online teenagers use social media sites, such as Facebook and Twitter (Lenhart et al., 2010), where users engage in digital writing by creating personal profiles, updating their statuses, exchanging messages, and sharing information with others. Indeed, as Lapp, Fisher, and Frey (2012) stated in the National Council of Teachers of English publication, *Voices from the Middle*: "[S]tudents are writing more than ever before . . . communicat[ing] through their blogs, emails, texting, and Facebook pages" (p. 7).

Yet, as many of the high school English educators who worked with us have noted, many students do not know how to transfer their everyday writing skills to academic contexts. Although students write and read constantly when they text, tweet, and update their statuses, they often do not view digital writing as related to academic writing—despite the fact that there are many similarities in these literacy practices (Greenhow & Robelia, 2009). In other words, "Teens write a lot, but they do not think of their emails, instant and text messages as writing. This disconnect matters because teens believe good writing is an essential skill for success and that more writing instruction at school would help them" (Lenhart et al., 2008). When they do write in class, many students view it as "an arduous task that causes them frustration, and their resulting essays often lack the quality desired by their teachers" (Lapp, Fisher, & Frey, 2012, p. 7).

Part of the difficulty is the fact that outside-of-school writing is not always the same as academic writing, particularly because outside-of-school writing sometimes adheres to different conventions than those of standardized English. What is often called "texting language" can include abbreviations (such as *brb* for *be right back*), initials (such as *gf* for *girlfriend*), and acronyms (such as *lol* for *laugh out loud*). It may also follow conventions such as placing more emphasis on brevity and less emphasis on standardized punctuation. Many secondary English educators are chagrined when their students' academic writing contains elements of texting language or follows texting conventions. But there are also many misconceptions about texting language and its effect on student communication.

First, as Crystal (2008) discussed, there is a widespread belief that texting relies heavily upon the use of abbreviations, initials, and acronyms. However, studies of large corpora of text messages have found that only about 10–20% of text messages show abbreviated forms. Our perceptions of texting language are likely skewed because of the salience of these forms. In other words, it is not that students use texting language all the time, but rather that it immediately stands out to us when they do; we therefore may perceive that the effect of texting language is larger than it actually is.

Texting language is also not as innovative as it is assumed to be. As Crystal (2008) explained, when it comes to the abbreviations, initials, and acronyms that texters use, many of these features "can be found in precomputer informal writing, dating back a hundred years or more." The use of *u* for *you* and *idk* for *I don't know* by today's students is no different from *IOU* for *I owe you* and *SWAK* for *sealed with a kiss* used by previous generations. Criticism has always surrounded the use of abbreviations, initials, and acronyms, but brevity is often an economical choice. Just as many texters write short messages to avoid extra charges, writers in earlier generations had similar financial concerns: Abbreviations, initials, and acronyms were routinely used in telegrams and letters, because telegraph companies charged by the number of letters in a message, and postage rates were based on weight. In fact, the first recorded use of *OMG* was in a typed letter sent during World War I by a British Navy admiral to Winston Churchill (Smithsonian, 2012).

Finally, although it is widely assumed that texting language is detrimental to student communication, much evidence suggests otherwise. Crystal (2008) noted the "extraordinary number of doom-laden prophecies" about the dangers and evils of texting. Just as it was once feared that the printing press would disrupt the "almost spiritual connection" between the writer and the page, and just as it was once feared that the typewriter would destroy the art of handwriting (Baron, 2012), many people continue to be wary of or to assume the worst about the effect of new technologies on the English language. In fact, fears that texting has a detrimental effect on literacy do not bear out upon investigation. "On the contrary," Crystal (2008) stated, "literacy improves. The latest studies . . . have found strong positive links between the use of text language and the skills underlying success in pre-teenage children. . . . The children who were better at spelling and writing used the most textisms" (para. 33). Although texting language often differs from standardized English, this difference does not mean that texting language is inherently wrong or that it is a slippery slope toward bad English. It is much more accurate to view texting language as an organic linguistic product, as "the latest manifestation of the human ability to be linguistically creative and to adapt language to suit the demands of diverse settings. . . . [I]n texting what we are seeing, in a small way, is language in evolution" (Crystal, 2008, para. 35).

Research that shows the benefit of digital writing on students' literacy development makes a case for secondary English educators to tap into the creative and pedagogical potential of technology. Educators can harness students' willingness to engage in texting, tweeting, blogging, and the like to engage them in writing as a multifaceted, variable, and flexible practice (Warschauer, 2007). These sorts of activities can be fun and creative, and they can break down communication barriers between students and educators, pointing out generational linguistic differences in a lighthearted way. As a secondary English educator who worked with us said, "I once had a student who wrote a poem using Facebook/texting language. The students had a good laugh when they realized I was the one who did not understand, and they had to translate for me." Texting language also can help illustrate the crucial point of register, discussed earlier in this chapter. Just as some of the conventions of academic English would be inappropriate and inefficient to use in a text, texting language is often too brief or imprecise to be used in an analytic essay. By guiding students to theorize and analyze how language evolves and how authors communicate differently based on audience and intent, secondary English educators can engage students in the study of English language and literature and can encourage them to write their own material that incorporates their own voice. We discuss these concepts further in Chapters 4 and 5.

Language Variation Is All Around Us

Just as language changes and varies, individual people communicate in unique ways. Our voice quality and language patterns are akin to our individual fingerprints. We refer to this concept as "respect for the idiolect," since *idiolect* is defined as a person's unique language patterns (Labov, 1972b). Attention to and respect for individual variation in linguistic style is part of fostering the academic and social development of every student, which is a primary goal of multicultural education.

BOX 2.7. FOR LINGUISTIC REFLECTION:
Language and Identity

When we do language, it can reveal something about our life experiences and how we want to present ourselves. What is your linguistic identity? Maybe you are the oldest sibling, the family historian, or the family comedian. Maybe you are a "girly" girl, nerd, or jock. Maybe you are put-together and formal, or casual and laid-back. Maybe you are still figuring out your identity! How has language played a role in your identity? The following questions can prompt reflection.

- Describe yourself in five words. What do these words say about you?
- How do you use language to reflect your personality? Your culture? Your family background?
- Has the language you use been accepted by others? Has it ever been challenged by your peers? By family members? By others? How have you dealt with these challenges?

Language often plays a more or less central role at different stages in our lives. Where we grew up, where we have lived, where we were educated, and where we now live can affect our language and speech styles, from vocabulary to pronunciation, grammar, and style. People who have lived in one neighborhood or city all their lives may sound like a textbook speaker of the area, or perhaps they have decided to not adopt features of local speech. People who move from place to place may acquire some of the linguistic characteristics of each place that they have lived, and others may use language in ways that are not easily placed.

One of the social factors that affects our language development and use is age. Among family and friends, on playgrounds, in churches, in neighborhoods, and at school, students can be skilled at communicating in ways that are tailored to different social situations and different social groups, particularly when it comes to peer interactions. Parents have an early influence over a child's language, but the peer group takes over as children get older and especially as they move into preadolescence. For example, noted linguist William Labov (1972a) studied the social networks of preadolescent African American boys in Harlem, New York. He found that these students used nonstandardized varieties of English in ways that earned them acceptance and praise among their peers, indicating the social and cultural functions of language.

Social class is another dimension that can relate to language use. In another study by Labov (1972b), he examined the *r* sound in New York City. At that time (and often today), many New Yorkers dropped the *r*'s in their words, pronouncing a word such as *bird* more like *boid*. To conduct an experiment, Labov chose three department stores that catered to differ-

BOX 2.8. AN EDUCATOR'S VIGNETTE: A Lesson on Code Switching

Julie Roos, 10th-Grade English Teacher,
AP English Language and Composition Teacher, and Debate Coach

I grew up almost preternaturally aware of the variations in English around me. I had a severe speech impediment as a young child, causing me to spend several hours a week with a specialist who drilled me on pronunciation. I was only 6 years old the first time I asked my mother why she said *worsh* instead of *wash*. Living in Pittsburgh, these variations were all around me, and my traditional schooling led me to believe that the language patterns of my household (*worsh, redd up, chipped ham, gumband, up 'ere, n'at*) were markers of inferiority, while the cottage industry of Pittsburghese paraphernalia and dictionaries argued that these variants should be used with regional pride. When I entered an undergraduate program in English Education, I knew that my inability to break myself of saying *needs washed* instead of *needs to be washed* and *keller* instead of *color* could lead to judgments about my ability to lead classrooms. But I also knew that the language I spoke is one that an entire region of the country uses and understands. If I wasn't going to make fun of my Philadelphian classmates for drinking *soda* and *wooder* (*water*), then I wasn't going to stand for them correcting me for *redding up* (*cleaning up*) my room. I had embraced my own linguistic nuances, and I was determined to let my students do so as well. While understanding the rules of academic English is important, understanding that academic English is only one code among many is even more vital.

My early formation as a proud speaker of a language variety was extremely important when I took my current job. I teach English at a large urban high school in North Las Vegas. Our student body is approximately 45% Hispanic, 45% African American and 10% everything else, with a significant number of European immigrants. Many of my students do not speak English as a primary language at home, and many are in the first two generations of their families to graduate high school. Our state requires all students to pass a writing proficiency test in order to graduate high school and emphasizes the use of academic language on the exam. I begin my students' preparation for the exam with a lesson on code switching, and I start with my own native code. Most of my students never consider that their teachers speak differently outside of school. They're used to hearing me speak in the code of academic English during class and debate practice, though I still can't break myself of saying *keller*, which causes them to look at me askance. Beginning a lecture with full-on "yinzer" (Pittsburgh) English makes them look at me differently, and they begin to look at their own language variations. Families migrate to Las Vegas from around the world, so there is quite a bit of language variation in each of my classes. Comparing their own language use to others' helps my students understand the wealth that language variation represents, and it even helps them on their tests—it's a win-win.

ent social classes: Saks Fifth Avenue (upper-class), Macy's (middle-class), and S. Klein (lower-class). Labov visited each store and asked a clerk for the location of an item that he knew to be on the fourth floor. When the clerk responded to his question by saying "fourth floor," Labov noted whether or not the clerk pronounced the *r* sound in the words *fourth* and *floor*. Then, by saying "Excuse me?" Labov was able to get the clerk to repeat *fourth floor*, this time using a more careful pronunciation. This experiment revealed two trends. First, the clerks' pronunciations of the *r* sounds correlated with the social status of the store they worked in. The higher the social status, the more likely the clerks were to pronounce *r*. Second, when they were asked the question a second time, speaking more carefully, the clerks who worked at S. Klein (the lower-status environment) were actually *more likely* than the clerks from either Macy's (middle-class) or Saks (upper-class) to pronounce their *r*'s. Labov reasoned that the clerks from S. Klein knew that many people viewed not pronouncing one's *r*'s as a lower-status behavior and were sensitive to that fact. Thus, when they were put into a social situation in which they felt compelled to speak more carefully, they were more likely than speakers of higher classes to use the more prestigious *r* sound more often.

It is not the case, however, that prestigious speech is always valued. One of Anne's former students described how, after graduating from college, she worked as a production controller on a nuclear aircraft carrier at a big shipyard. Until that point, she said, her life had been "pretty Ivory Tower—upper-middle-class, White, Midwestern family, boarding school, a great college." When she began working in the shipyard, however, she was frequently picked on for using big words and sounding like a "snob." A supervisor even mentioned originally not wanting to hire her. "When pressed as to why," she said, "I could never get a straight answer. I think the fact is, even though I did a fine job, I didn't fit in enough for them, and a large part of it was the way in which I communicate." As this student's quote reveals, while nonstandardized English is often stigmatized because it is predominantly used by working-class Americans (Wolfram, 1980), stigma can also surround language that is seen as being "too proper." For this reason, people of a higher social class sometimes may use nonstandardized features for emphasis, for effect, to fit in, to add "color" to their speech, or to resonate with an audience; lawyers and politicians are often an excellent illustration of this point (Kendall & Wolfram, 2009). People who use nonstandardized varieties of English are also often viewed as being more personable, friendly, down-home, and casual than people who speak very standardly. Some speakers can easily shift the way they talk, while for others, making those linguistic shifts can prove daunting. Social class interacts with language use in complex ways, and understanding these nuances is beneficial for educators and students, especially those in diverse classrooms and schools.

In addition to age and social class, gender can correspond with language use. Gender-based language differences are not innate but rather are learned. Due to social pressures and norms, girls and women are often socialized to speak and act in ways that are viewed as being more polite (Eckert & McConnell-Ginet, 2003). As a result, they may avoid using features such as *ain't* or swear words that boys and men sometimes embrace. At the same time, girls and women are often leaders of the pack when it comes to creating, learning, and spreading new and innovative linguistic features (Eckert & McConnell-Ginet, 2003).

Research on language and gender in educational contexts has found that boys are encouraged to express themselves more frequently and openly; boys are more often called on in class (and by name), although they also are more likely to get into trouble (Sadker & Sadker, 1994). Much classroom discord is undoubtedly due to verbal conflicts and to miscommunications between boys and educators. The majority of educators in the United States are women, and they likely have certain notions about what is polite and acceptable that may be informed by their own standpoints and worldviews. The relative lack of men as teachers, especially in primary schools, can leave boys without gender-specific linguistic role models at the very time when language patterns are being taught and codified (Hutchings et al., 2008). It is also important to take gender into account when we consider how other linguistic behaviors, such as silence and loudness, speaking up in class, acting out in class, and teasing and bullying, might be used by boys and girls in a given classroom or school.

Language is deeply emblematic of our identities and backgrounds, and as a result the ways that educators interpret and respond to students' language use may directly and deeply affect that young person. Speakers are often sensitive to negative ideologies about their language and may even interpret criticism as a personal attack (Lippi-Green, 2011). Sometimes, in the face of disapproval or correction, students may choose to remain true to the language that feels most comfortable to them in order to sound trustworthy and authentic. Other students who are critiqued for their language without sufficient explanation as to why and how to address the issue may become overwhelmed, confused, and discouraged. They may also lose confidence in the learning process, their own abilities, their educators, and school in general (Labov, 1995). Not all students will strive to speak in standardized ways at all times—nor should they, as wholesale assimilation and homogeneity is not a goal of multicultural education. It is therefore important for educators to understand the deep and abiding connections between language and identity and how they can affect behavior in academic settings.

LINGUISTIC TRUTH #3: LANGUAGE DIFFERENCES ARE NOT LANGUAGE DEFICITS

Language differences are not the same as language deficits. Language is always changing and is part and parcel of social interaction. As a result, language differences arise. These differences are normal and natural because language change itself is a normal and natural process (Labov, 1972b). Patterned differences in sound, grammar, and word choice help distinguish what linguists call *language varieties*, which vary by region, personal background, gender, social class, age, race/ethnicity, and more. Any language variety is just as logical and internally consistent as another, and, just like standardized English, nonstandardized varieties of English are rule-governed and predictable in their linguistic structure and use.

Earlier we discussed the fact that, in this book, we use the term *language variety*, which is roughly comparable to the term *dialect*. Dialect is a term that is commonly used, but it is also often used pejoratively. Consider the following sentence: "The kids in the neighborhood don't really speak English; they speak a dialect" (quoted in Wolfram & Schilling-Estes, 2006, p. 3). This sentence represents the idea that a dialect is inherently somehow worse because of its linguistic differences, which is a common misperception. As we have noted, if any language variety or linguistic feature is viewed as being "better" or "worse" than any other, it is only because people have decided that it carries a certain social standing. As linguist Steven Pinker (2012) explained, "The choice of *isn't* over *ain't*, *dragged* over *drug*, and *can't get any* over *can't get no* did not emerge from a weighing of their inherent merits, but from the historical accident that the first member of each pair was used in the dialect spoken around London when the written language became standardized. If history had unfolded differently, today's correct forms could have been incorrect and vice versa." "Historical accidents," as Pinker put it, are similarly responsible for many spellings and pronunciations in standardized English that are odd and sometimes confusing, as anyone who has tried to learn or teach words like *bought*, *known*, *primer*, or *segue* will understand firsthand.

Despite these linguistic realities, language varieties are often stigmatized. Linguistic research has unfortunately found that listeners routinely perceive speakers of standardized English as being smarter, of a higher status, and as having more positive personality traits than speakers of nonstandardized English varieties (Lippi-Green, 2011). We all make assumptions sometimes,

BOX 2.9. FOR LINGUISTIC REFLECTION: Language Variation

We often have strong feelings about the types of language we like best. Where do these perceptions come from? Some of the following questions are food for individual thought, while others can be used as classroom discussion starters.

- What type of language variation do you find interesting? Where do you hear different types of language: in your neighborhood? On television? In music? Online?
- Can people tell where you're from by the way you talk? What do they notice about how you talk?
- Has a parent, guardian, or other adult ever tried to correct your speech? What things were they successful in changing, or not?
- Are there things that you try to change in the speech of others? What about your own speech?
- Do you think that trying to change others' speech is a question of ethics, etiquette, or neither? In what situations do you find it acceptable to correct another person's language? When do you find it unacceptable?
- Listen to the podcast "Should You Point Out Errors?" by Grammar Girl (2011). She discussed several considerations for people who want to point out someone's grammatical error—but, she stated, she doesn't point out other people's errors herself. Do you and Grammar Girl agree or disagree?

but drawing conclusions about people based simply on how they talk can lead to false judgments, stereotypes, and discrimination. The tenets of multiculturalism challenge us to critically examine these notions, however, and to see differences as part of the natural spectrum of humanity. We therefore advocate for linguistic awareness in classrooms, schools, communities, and society. Our model of linguistic awareness, grounded in multicultural education, appreciates the rich and varied backgrounds and identities that students bring with them to classrooms and schools and views this diversity not as a deficit but as a resource.

SUPPORTING LINGUISTICALLY AND CULTURALLY DIVERSE STUDENTS

Attitudes and beliefs about language are tightly woven into our ideas about teaching and learning and into our pedagogical practices (Reaser, 2006; Reaser & Wolfram, 2007). As we discussed in the previous section, society often privileges certain types of English and stigmatizes those that are nonmainstream. Classrooms, schools, and even education itself as a social institution are not immune from the effects of these beliefs and attitudes. Within a mainstream educational context that privileges standardized English, it is important to consider the potential effects on students who speak nonstandardized varieties of English.

Linguistic differences, which often co-occur with cultural differences, can put nonstandardized English-speaking students at a very different social and educational starting point than students who come to school already speaking standardized English. Students who are already familiar with standardized English may be seen as being more "promising" and may receive more educational opportunities (Charity Hudley & Mallinson, 2011). In contrast, students who do not come to school already speaking the mainstream variety may face deep pressure to assimilate and may be perceived to be less intelligent or less capable if they do not (Wolfram, 1998). Some traditional sources imply that if people are educated and are native speakers of English, they could not possibly also use nonstandardized varieties of English. This idea is harmful to impart, particularly given that some of the most highly educated and successful figures in history—from presidents and other politicians to teachers, artists, novelists, and ministers—have used language variation when communicating some of the great messages of our time. Rather than pressuring them to erase linguistic differences, it is important to honor the backgrounds of nonstandardized English-speaking students, providing the social support and academic tools they need to succeed.

In line with language standards, such as the Common Core Standards and those set by the National Council of Teachers of English, teaching students to understand the English language in its many forms and varieties is an effective and culturally responsive model of English education (National Council of Teachers of English, 2003). Rather than glossing over language variation, we emphasize the importance of explicitly instructing students as to the norms and conventions of standardized English while building their understanding of nonstandardized varieties of English. In the special issue of *English Journal* (Lindblom, 2011), English educators discuss how they have explored the richness of language when teaching literature and language arts.

The ability to communicate effectively with respect to register, context, and audience enhances a student's linguistic awareness, flexibility, and versatility. As Smitherman and Villanueva (2003) noted, real-world educational and professional situations bring together speakers of different languages and language varieties. Students who are able to navigate this diversity are well positioned to succeed in our multicultural society.

In our four-pronged multicultural approach to English education (Charity Hudley & Mallinson, 2011), it is critical to specifically discuss with students the concept of *standardized English*. Students will become aware that standardized English is considered to be the variety of privilege and prestige, a status it has acquired due to the influence of powerful decision

BOX 2.10. AN EDUCATOR'S VIGNETTE: Preserving Students' Heart Language

Linda Krause, 9th-Grade English Teacher

I am becoming more and more convinced that many of my students are fighting to preserve their "heart language" in the only way they know how—with typical teenage defiance. When my students' feet first hit the floor of my 9th-grade English classroom at the beginning of the year, conversations frequently included at least one emphatically delivered *ain't* complete with a "whaddaya gonna do 'bout it" look. I ignored them all. Finally, one curious kid volunteered, "You gonna let me say that? *Ain't* ain't a real word, you know."

"Really?" I said, "What makes a word real? It's in the dictionary, you used it in a sentence, and it communicated meaning."

The room went silent. Shocked faces stared.

"Our last year's English teacher said it wasn't a real word," a different student finally interjected. "We said it all the time to bug her."

"You use it like a real word. I get what you say." I shrugged.

Uh oh, I thought; I didn't want to undermine the last teacher's credibility, so I hastened to explain that *ain't* is not a word used in standard English, but then they weren't speaking standard English anyway; they were speaking Appalachian. That was a novel twist, and they loved it.

After we had The Conversation, a mystery started to clear up for me: Why, after multiple explicit grammar mini-lessons, did students continue to repeatedly make the same errors in their writing? Forget the mini-lessons; it was time for me to use a new tactic. I started highlighting grammatical "mistakes" and writing "Please translate" next to them. To my great surprise, students could suddenly self-correct the grammar, although sometimes they would frown in extreme concentration and ask for help.

Apparently, these students, all placed in my class because of their supposedly low English skills, could shift between standard and Appalachian English with a lot more fluency than I realized. They were making a choice, albeit unconscious, to stubbornly cling to their own English variation.

Were my views accurate? It was time for an open-ended survey. Only one student would admit to saying *ain't* just to irritate me, but there were other revelations. The hard-liners' opinion was, "Nobody's going to stop me from saying it." Middle-grounders said they spoke standard English more in English class than other classes because they wanted to pass or thought they would get in trouble if they didn't. However, there seemed to be a fair number who assess the effects of using standard versus Appalachian English and adjust accordingly. Overall, students expressed being comfortable in my class, and some felt much more confident in their ability to communicate. That confidence seems to have arisen from honoring their dialect's grammar rather than treating it as wrong.

Awareness and acceptance go a long way toward eliciting cooperation and engagement. I don't hear *ain't* from nearly as many students as I used to. I might start saying it myself—I sorta, you know, like, kinda miss it.

makers, including dictionary writers, curriculum writers, testing companies, and politicians. Second, we advocate the importance of explicitly teaching students the norms and conventions of standardized English while also helping students learn the differences between standardized English and the languages and language varieties they bring with them from home. Third, we advocate that educators learn about students' linguistic backgrounds and communication styles. To help all students achieve the goal of becoming communicatively competent, it is important for educators to be able to identify language variation and approach language differences in culturally responsive and sociolinguistically informed ways. Finally, we believe that educators who hold positive language attitudes can help all students understand language differences. With awareness and respect, all educators and students can develop an appreciation for the richness and beauty of language, used by others and ourselves.

CONCLUSION

With an understanding of the three linguistic truths that we presented in this chapter, secondary English educators are able to value and build on their students' home languages and language varieties as they help their students learn the norms and conventions of standardized English. As students build their linguistic awareness, they can use this knowledge and information to understand the communication of others as well as to make their own informed judgments and decisions about how to use language. Our linguistic truths parallel many language standards that are recommended or adopted in educational settings, which encourage educators to teach students the norms and conventions of standardized varieties of English *and* help them learn how to express themselves, according to different social circumstances and communicative goals.

In Box 2.11 on pp. 39–41, sociolinguist and professor Dr. Jeffrey Reaser describes his experience as a former high school English teacher who came to appreciate the centrality of language to the mission of secondary English education. He conceptualizes English Language Arts as a three-legged stool, consisting of language, literature, and writing. In fact, his metaphor carries us forward in this book. In Chapter 3, we advocate for secondary English educators to have conversations about language and culture. In Chapter 4, we examine the merits of studying language variation in literature. In Chapter 5, we empower students to find their own voices and tell their own stories, both in conventional writing and in digital writing. In Reaser's metaphor, like a three-legged stool, each topic relates to the other and is central in the quest to promote the success of all students in secondary English environments.

BOX 2.11. A SOCIOLINGUIST'S VIGNETTE: My Linguistic Journey as an English Educator

Dr. Jeffrey Reaser,
Associate Professor of English at North Carolina State University

I took the long way to sociolinguistics, and in many ways, I tried to resist its pull long after it had thoroughly captured my imagination. My heart has always rested in education. As a kindergartener, I wrote in my journal that I wanted to be a "teacher or a garbage man" (please excuse my gendered language as a 5-year-old). English classes were my most persistent struggle in public school, and by about 6th grade, I had succumbed to the seemingly coordinated message from teachers and parents about my future in engineering. Everyone was shocked, understandably, when I announced in 12th grade that I intended to be a high school English teacher.

I had no knowledge of linguistics when I enrolled in my required "History of the English Language" class as a junior in college. Fifteen years later, I have enough vivid memories of astonishing revelations about language from that class to fill twice the space I'm allotted here. Though I was intrigued by the application of scientific principles to language, I resisted linguistics' temptation long enough to dip my toes into teaching high school. Eventually, I gave in to an MA and a PhD. Halfway through the latter, I realized, sorrowfully, that I was becoming a linguist instead of a teacher. As I attempted to step away from the academy and back into the classroom, my dissertation advisor suggested that I combine my interest in sociolinguistics with my passion for education. For almost a decade now, I have been happily working to increase the presence of linguistics in public education. I have had a few successes along the way, and my brief recounting of them here will not allow proper recognition of academic colleagues and classroom teachers who have contributed to these collaborative projects.

The work that has garnered the most attention is my coauthored *Voices of North Carolina* dialect awareness curriculum (Reaser & Wolfram, 2007), which aligns with the state-mandated Standard Course of Study for 8th-grade social studies, where students explore the history and culture of North Carolina. To a linguist, language is one of the state's richest but least publicized cultural resources and one of the most emblematic badges of its history. The multimedia curriculum examines basic sociolinguistic tenets as it explores seven dialects or languages of North Carolina. Virtually all 8th-grade curricular goals can be examined or reinforced through the linguistic lens: settlement, geography, migration, legislative policy, citizenship, and economic development. For example, the curriculum explores the lingering linguistic effects of the early English settlers in the Pamlico Sound region and of the Scots-Irish in the mountains. Examining the current state of American Indian languages reinforces the devastating effects of "civilization" legislation, a knowledge that builds empathy in students as they consider "English Only" policies threatening Spanish speakers. My argument is simple: Any treatment of the history and culture of North Carolina that does not explore its linguistic diversity is woefully incomplete. Ours is the first state-based curriculum in the United States and is further distinguished by being designed so that teachers without a background in linguistics are able to teach it effectively as measured by gains in students' language knowledge and improving about language variation (see Reaser, 2006). Because we hope for widespread implementation, we disseminate the curriculum and all related materials for free via the NC State linguistics website.

A second project I was lucky enough to be involved with was a curriculum for high school language arts accompanying the 3-hour documentary, *Do You Speak American?* (MacNeil & Cran, 2005). Under the aegis of the Center for Applied Linguistics, we created materials that facilitated use of this rich resource in classrooms and professional development settings. We listened closely to teachers, who preferred thematic units to a traditional chronological approach, and created a curriculum enmeshing the topics they found most compelling—including communicative choices and personal style, perspectives on spoken and written language, regional dialects, Spanish and Hispanicized English, and African American English—with sociolinguistic perspectives. Since the curriculum was designed for a national audience, we used as a framework content standards from the National Council of Teachers of English and the National Council for the Social Studies. Like the North Carolina curriculum, these materials are available free via the web.

These are just two of the many projects I've undertaken in an attempt to integrate linguistics into the public school curriculum. With my graduate students, I have also worked on a curriculum that explores the history of English alongside British literature; a curriculum that teaches about language, gender, and ideology via canonical American literature; a curriculum that scientifically explores formal grammar; and curricula for ESL instruction based on pragmatics or enhanced through information on dialect variation. While these curricula remain in less than finalized form, many materials from them have been eagerly sought out and widely distributed to teachers.

Through these and other projects, I feel I have made some headway integrating linguistic information into public schools. While I do not wish to diminish the value of quality packaged lessons and units, it seems to me that these "add-on" curricula are bandages to a much larger issue, namely that linguistics remains outside the mainstream public school environment, and in many cases, outside of teacher education and professional development. I like to think of English Language Arts as a three-legged stool, with one leg being literature, the second writing, and the third language (I cannot claim to have originated this analogy). The stool is useless unless all three legs are of equal length. At my university, students studying to become secondary English teachers take 13 English classes beyond first-year writing. Of these, eight are required literature classes, two are electives, and the remaining three are one each of film, literacy, and linguistics. It's clear we are sending teachers into classrooms with stools of dubious balance. I see my most valuable contributions as far more local than global. With only anecdotes for data, I am convinced that my most direct impact in the schools arises through the future teachers I am lucky enough to teach, many of whom leave our program spreading the linguistics gospel in their classrooms and schools. It is in my privileged role as teacher of teachers that I feel, finally, a meshing of two worlds into one lucid whole. My dream is that one day, all teachers of all subjects will view language as something that ought to be studied scientifically, and that those teachers are then, over time, able to wipe out the folklore associated with dialect that is damaging to so many students. To this end, I am happy to be one of many friends, colleagues, and, yes, former students, engaged in teaching about language variation. Sociolinguistics finally claimed me, but I'm still first and foremost "just" a teacher.

CHAPTER 3

Language and Culture: Having Courageous Conversations

"How can I teach my students to speak and write so that they can sound educated and cultured?" Many educators have asked us a form of this question as they strive to help their students navigate the languages and language varieties they bring with them from home and the language they are expected to use in school. Our answer is that, as educators, we must consider culture conceptually and practically. We must have concrete explanations for and discussions about what culture is, our classroom culture, the cultures of our students, and how our cultural expectations are intertwined with our teaching in order to fully appreciate its relationship to language. This approach to language and culture dovetails with the principles of multicultural education, which explicitly values diversity and supports teaching that takes into account cultural context (Banks & Banks, 2007; Gay, 1994). This approach also parallels academic research known as New Literacy Studies, including scholarship by Gee (1996), Kirkland (2010), and Gilyard (2011), which recognizes that society, culture, community, and family deeply influence how an individual acquires and develops language and literacy.

According to the National Council of Teachers of English and the International Reading Association (1996), it is important to help students "develop an understanding of and respect for diversity in language use, patterns, and dialects across cultures, ethnic groups, geographic regions, and social roles" (p. 41). The organizations explained, "Language is a powerful medium through which we develop social and cultural understanding, and the need to foster this understanding is growing increasingly urgent as our culture becomes more diverse . . . . Schools are responsible for creating a climate of respect for the variety of languages that students speak and the variety of cultures from which they come" (pp. 41–42). Similar rationales are given in the Common Core State Standards Initiative (2012c): Students who are college and career ready in reading, writing, speaking, listening, and language "actively seek to understand other perspectives and cultures through reading and listening, and they are able to communicate effectively with people of varied backgrounds" (p. 7).

Language is a vehicle through which speakers also express their cultural beliefs and participate in cultural practices. In this chapter, we delve into the relationship between language and culture to meet several goals: to guide secondary English educators and students to develop linguistic awareness and cultural understanding; to enable secondary English educators to understand the different forms of linguistic capital that students bring to the classroom; to better equip secondary English educators to honor students' cultural and linguistic diversity in praxis; and to prepare secondary English educators to hold important conversations about language and culture in their classrooms and schools, in ways that reflect a culturally and linguistically responsive pedagogy.

LANGUAGE IS CULTURE, CULTURE IS LANGUAGE

According to Erickson (2007), culture is a socially acquired system of meaning. In this broad definition of culture, cultural differences can surface not only with regard to race/ethnicity and national origin but also along the lines of social class, gender, sexual orientation, religion, age, rurality versus urbanity, and more. To a degree, there is a U.S. *macroculture*: For instance, as Americans we generally value the ideas of equality and individual opportunity (Banks & Banks, 2007). Yet, there is also much cultural variability. According to Banks and Banks, any macroculture consists of various *microcultures*. Microcultures often share aspects of the macroculture, but they also might not overlap, as members may hold beliefs, values, and practices that are different from broader society.

Cultural variability and linguistic variability go hand in hand, and language is a tool for expressing the elements that make up a given microculture. Consider the following words and phrases: *cable*, *cast off*, and *gauge*. At first, this list might not seem characteristic of any specific microculture. But what if we added *purl*, *skein*, and *swatch*? Now that we have read the rest of the list, we may realize that the words are well known by people who knit; that is, they are part of the jargon of a knitting microculture. People outside that microculture, however, might not understand the meaning of those words or how exactly they are being used. Classroom microcultures also rely on language for their expression. In *The Skin That We Speak: Thoughts on Language and Culture in the Classroom*, Delpit and Dowdy (2008) explained that language is a primary vehicle for reflecting and transmitting culture. For instance, what counts in classrooms as being funny, as opposed to insolent? What sounds direct or indirect, challenging or passive, or even passive-aggressive? What constitutes a lie versus a story or make-believe? These and many other linguistic elements are part of classroom microcultures. Some linguistic elements may be shared across microcultures, but others may vary and may not be shared or understood by all members.

In classrooms and schools, the cultural bases for our linguistic assumptions are too often not discussed, and conversations about our linguistic expectations for students tend to be held indirectly, if at all. As Banks and Banks (2007) noted, it is important to have discussions about invisible as well as visible aspects of culture to help avoid the "cultural misunderstandings, conflicts, and institutionalized discrimination" that can occur when cultural differences are misinterpreted (p. 7). The challenge in classrooms and schools is to discuss culture and language explicitly, so that educators and students can understand the norms that may differ from classroom to classroom and the cultural and linguistic beliefs, values, and practices of educators and students.

To start the conversation about culture, Figure 3.1 provides a model for how to conceptualize various microcultures and how they may or may not overlap with the broader U.S. macroculture (adapted from Banks & Banks, 2007, p. 11). As a classroom exercise, students and educators can fill out the circles with labels that indicate some of the many microcultures they belong to. Perhaps someone in the class belongs to a knitting club, as in our earlier example, or is a member of a sports team or a Scout troop. Students may belong to microcultures based on their age, ethnicity, social class, religion, or other characteristics. Or perhaps they belong to microcultures for runners, bikers, vegetarians, science fiction readers, videogame enthusiasts, NASCAR fans, cheerleaders, band members, or people who love Disney World. The options are as varied as the personalities and backgrounds of those in the class. Students can keep their microcultures to themselves or share them with the class. Group discussions about microcultures should be framed for students as conversations in which everyone respects what each other has to say. Each student will participate in many different microcultures, and no student should single out another for participation or lack of participation in a given microculture. It will be important to make clear to students that this exercise is a way to honor each other and learn about the cultural diversity of their classmates.

After establishing the range of variation across microcultures, a direct parallel can be made to variety in language. Educators and students can consider such questions as: What sorts of everyday words and phrases are used in your microcultures? What jargon is used in your microcultures that other people might not understand? How do you like to communicate with people in your microcultures? Do you communicate in person? Through letters or notes? Via phone or computer? Through email, texts, Facebook, or Twitter? Using these questions as discussion starters or as essay prompts can increase students' awareness of how they use language within cultural spheres. It also can offer a glimpse into students' linguistic worlds and com-

FIGURE 3.1. United States Macroculture and Microcultures

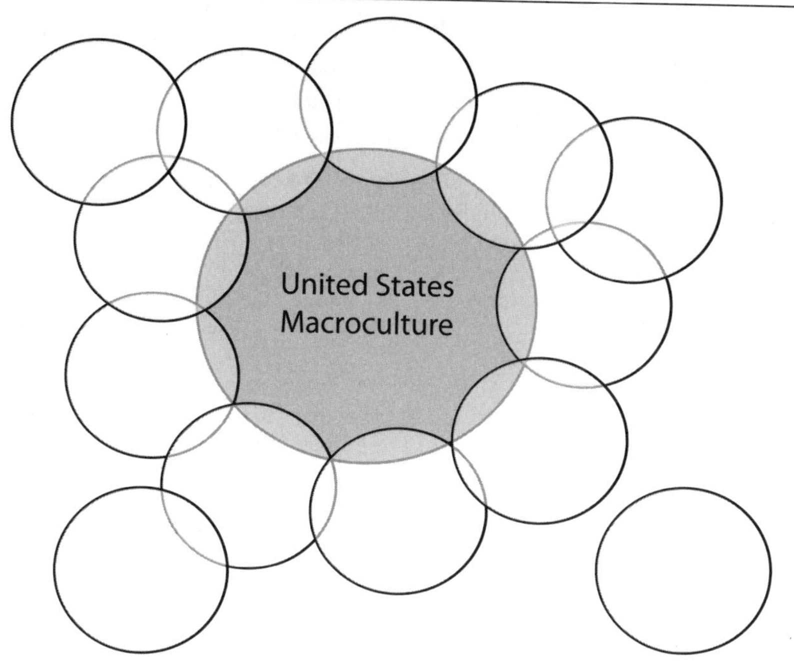

munities of practice, a term coined by Lave and Wenger (1991) to refer to groups of people who are mutually engaged in particular tasks. As individuals engage with each other within communities of practice, their actions, including common ways of speaking, shape and are shaped by their social identities. The microcultures activity therefore emphasizes the range of communication practices that are used in different segments of society, and it communicates the message that language is an immediate and powerful way that we present ourselves to the world.

In Box 3.1 on pp. 46–47, a former middle school language arts teacher described how he was able to connect with his students and begin to overcome cultural divides when he realized that it was necessary to understand not only his students' backgrounds but also his own. Narrative is a powerful tool. By sharing their stories, educators and students can bridge differences and build connections.

COMMUNICATIVE BURDENS: A CULTURAL CHALLENGE

Despite the fact that communication is a necessary part of daily interactions, it is not always a smooth process. Any communicative exchange requires at

BOX 3.1. AN EDUCATOR'S VIGNETTE: Not in *Joyzee* Anymore

Christopher Justice,
Lecturer at the University of Baltimore
and Former 7th-Grade Language Arts Teacher

Although my professors in the University of New Mexico's Secondary English Education program prepared me well for the challenges of teaching middle and high school English, they didn't prepare me for this.

After completing that program, I landed a job at an Albuquerque middle school, teaching 7th-grade language arts. Albuquerque, like many Western cities, is neatly divided into essentially four squares. I lived in the northeast, a middle-class area that became more white-collar as one drove toward the foothills of the majestic Sandia Mountains. My school was 45 minutes southwest across the city, located south of Central Avenue. Parts of Albuquerque south of Central were known as "The War Zone" because of their gang activity, poverty, and crime. This world was, for me—at the time, a 25-year-old, middle-class, White guy from New Jersey—another planet.

While driving to school, I often saw roadrunners, jackrabbits, burrowing owls, and coyotes along the panoramic horizon. Even New Jersey's zoos didn't have those creatures. Stray dogs roamed the streets surrounding my school, and sometimes tumbleweeds rolled along the mesas. The setting was a clash between *Stand By Me* and Georgia O'Keefe. Drive-bys were common too. I remember one student describing the details of that gang ritual and then, later that evening, hearing those same details on the news. The congruence was eerie because this kid was barely 13 years old, 100 pounds, and 4 feet tall. I clearly wasn't in the comfortable suburb of Milltown, New Jersey anymore.

Unfortunately, the chaos outside my school often reflected the chaos inside my classroom. Like many first-year teachers, I struggled to get through to my students. They rarely brought books or supplies to class; they asked irrelevant questions; they disliked the readings and assignments; they failed to grasp basic concepts about language and writing; and they perceived our classroom as a place to socialize, not to learn. Although I had started with enough idealism to solve world hunger, many of my students received Ds and Fs that first quarter. Consequently, our assistant principal visited me to have a "sit down." She was angry and reminded me that most of the 7th-graders at my school were reading at a 3rd-grade level. She ripped into my failure to adjust to their learning styles and put me on the defensive. She offered few suggestions and told me to change my teaching style or there would be consequences. I had about an ounce of idealism left.

What I soon learned changed everything: My students were having a hard time culturally acclimating themselves to, of all things, *my* speech. It wasn't necessarily my teaching, but *how* I spoke that threw them off. Some students complained I spoke too quickly. Others were more specific: My pronunciations, such as *wooder* (*water*), *cawfee* (*coffee*), and *muzam* (*museum*), launched them into fits of laughter and secured their perception of me as The Other. Now I understood the seemingly random snickers. Instead of a teacher marginalizing minority students because of their speech, these students were marginalizing me—now, for the first time in my life, a minority teacher—because of mine. The irony was profound but liberating. I suddenly felt the way many marginalized students must feel whose speech patterns don't conform to "standard" English. As one of the few White males in the entire school, I was The Outsider. In fact, just about all of my students were Hispanic, Native American, or African American. I was foolish not to realize and embrace these differences sooner, but in hindsight, I'm lucky I did after only 3 months.

I quickly adapted. I shared stories about my background growing up in the New York metropolitan area, which they enjoyed. I interacted more with my students and inquired more about their interests. I spoke more slowly in class, making sure silence became an integral part of my diction. Eventually, our classroom environment changed: They followed directions more closely, asked interesting questions, and engaged with their assignments. While I'd love to think that, through my savvy pedagogical acumen, I transformed all my students into highly literate, Pulitzer Prize–winning authors, nothing like that happened. Much more progress could have been made. No miracles occurred, but we did get along better, and the learning environment became more productive.

What else did I learn from this experience? Plenty. I learned that *my* cultural background matters as much as my students' and that not only is *what* I say important, but *how* I say it may be more important. I also realized the power of discourse and that my speech encompasses a diversity of traits beyond just words and sentences, including volume, pace, accent, syntax, values, assumptions, and ideologies. Perhaps most significantly, I learned that culture and discourse are intimately related. These 7th-graders also taught me that, in the classroom, adaptation is everything. I've been adapting to my students ever since and am a better teacher—and better person—for doing so.

least two participants, but there is no guarantee as to how this exchange will take place and whether the communication will be effective. Lippi-Green (2011) discussed the concept of *communicative burden*. In a given communicative exchange, if both parties take on equal responsibility for understanding each other, then they share the communicative burden, as they are both seeking to understand what the other person is saying.

It is also possible for communicative burdens to be unequally distributed. According to Lippi-Green, in situations where there is a perceived language barrier between a person with a so-called mainstream accent and a person with a so-called nonmainstream accent, the person with the nonmainstream accent is often expected to do more work to help the other person understand. This concept means that people with nonmainstream accents can carry more than their fair share of the communicative burden. This inequality can happen in situations where someone's accent directly causes a misunderstanding, but it can also happen when other people have a bias against that accent. As Lippi-Green (2011) explained, when speakers of mainstream varieties encounter an unfamiliar accent, "the first decision they make is whether or not they are going to accept their responsibility in the act of communication" (p. 70). Some speakers make the decision to accept mutual responsibility and share the communicative burden. Others may hear an unfamiliar accent and immediately try to relieve themselves of the communicative burden by saying, "I can't understand you"—and sometimes what they mean is "I don't want to try to understand you," or, in a more extreme case, "I don't want to understand you."

Disproportionate conversational burdens can be particularly challenging when they involve hierarchies of age and status, such as between adults and children or between teachers and students. Due to the power dynamics in school and classroom settings, students may interpret conversational inequality in different ways (Christenbury, 1996). Some students may feel that it is their duty to take on a heavier conversational burden and may strive to solve their apparent communication problems with no questions asked. Others may feel shame or embarrassment if they believe that educators and peers cannot understand them. Some students may be offended when an educator or a peer claims, "I can't understand you," particularly if it seems as though this statement is a shortcut for "I don't want to understand you." If certain types of language are devalued, what messages are communicated to students who use them? These students may feel that their language is devalued and, by proxy, that their identities are devalued as well.

Many people, including students, find it difficult to accept the message that they have to suppress part of their linguistic identity to operate within mainstream culture (Richardson, 2009; see also Richardson's vignette, Box 5.9, pp. 132–133). Even if they are indirect messages, the idea that a speaker must accommodate to others linguistically and culturally in order to succeed can be distressing or offensive. When communication breakdowns occur, some speakers may work harder to help listeners understand them. Sometimes they may even raise their voices to be heard. Other times, they may silence themselves, perhaps because they think that other people can't comprehend what they are saying or because they have decided that they do not want to be understood. Lippi-Green's explanation that people who use language in nonmainstream ways often carry more than their fair share of the communicative burden can help educators analyze how this issue affects students in classrooms and schools.

BOX 3.2. FOR LINGUISTIC REFLECTION:
Communicative Burdens

Many teachers have had a shy student who sits in the back of the room and seems disengaged, as well as the overactive student who is always talking out of turn. These types of situations could be due to linguistic or communicative differences. Some questions for educators to think about include:

- What communicative burdens might my students face?
- Do all of the students in my classroom seem to share the communicative burden equally, or do some students seem to shoulder more than others?
- How might my students react if they felt that they had to bear a disproportionate responsibility to make themselves understood?
- What would a classroom look like in which the communicative burden was mutually shared?

Cultural and Linguistic Capital

Unequal communicative burdens are not simply a linguistic issue; they also can reflect broader cultural differences. Sometimes a classroom microculture may conflict with or contradict the beliefs, values, and practices of students' own microcultures, and there may be different cultural expectations for how students should communicate and behave. For example, as Carter (2007) analyzed, if some African American students push harder to assimilate to mainstream academic culture in order to succeed in school, which may include trying to assimilate linguistically, they may feel forced to pull away from their home communities. Kinloch (2010) interviewed two young African American men from New York City, Phillip and Khaleeq, on this topic. As Phillip explained, "It's like telling me I gotta take off my culture and identity when I leave my hood and go to a place that don't care about me. Like schools. How can I leave me and my Black English home? I'm nobody's traitor" (p. 104). Similarly, Khaleeq stated, "Taking away how students talk is taking away the students' culture, it's saying that the students' language is not correct, is inferior to the dominant culture, and incorrect in comparison to others" (p. 122). The quotes allude to the concept of "keeping it real," often used by African Americans to express the idea that even though the norms of White society prevail in many social institutions, internal respect for African American culture, which includes respect for African American English, is essential (Carter, 2007).

Some African American educators may feel similar tensions related to identity and culture (Carter, 2007; Howard, 2010; Smitherman, 2000). The feeling of being pulled in different linguistic and cultural directions has been conceptualized by some African American scholars as a "double consciousness" (Du Bois, 1903) or as having "double voices" (Balester, 1993, p. 15). In these situations, many speakers feel forced to choose one linguistic or cultural mode of expression over another to succeed in a mainstream world. Others might embrace the duality and view it as an extra linguistic resource. Research has found that some African American educators use both standardized English and African American English, in order to build rapport with their African American students (Foster, 1989). It is valuable to have educators who can discuss with students the social and cultural contexts surrounding language variation and the significance of encountering multiple linguistic varieties at school (Charity Hudley & Mallinson, 2011).

Students and educators from other historically marginalized cultural groups have faced similar linguistic situations. Native Americans have tragically described the losses they experienced due to attending boarding schools in the 1800s, where students were forced to assimilate to White norms (Locklear, 2011). Students from Appalachia and the South also sometimes feel that the culture and language of their home communities clashes with that of their classroom or school (DeYoung, 1995; Locklear, 2011; Purcell-Gates, 1997). These students may begin to feel disconnected from education, which can affect their ideas about achievement and the opportunities they seek out in life. Novelist Denise Giardina recalled, "When I was in school [in the 1950s and 1960s] . . . we were never told there were Appalachian writers. We didn't read stories set in the mountains. And Appalachian people were not in the history books. . . . Other places were where things happened. I had no idea I could be a writer" (Douglass, 2006, p. 246). Similarly, North Carolina–born novelist Lee Smith recalled, "When I was growing up in the mountains [of North Carolina] we were always told that culture existed somewhere else, and when the time came, we were going to be sent off to get some" (Locklear, 2011, p. 170).

The unfortunate reality is that culture clashes can be reflected in school settings on an institutional level. According to Heath (1983), "the school is not a neutral objective arena; it is an institution which has the goal of changing people's values, skills, and knowledge bases" (p. 367). For students who come from cultural backgrounds that are farther afield from dominant school and classroom culture, they may be expected to change to fit in, whereas students from middle-class or upper-class backgrounds may already fit in. According to Bourdieu (1991), the culture of dominant social institutions, such as schools, is closely aligned with middle-class and upper-class culture. As a result, the same habits and practices that are valued in middle- and upper-class settings are typically valued in schools. These habits and practices are embedded in what many theorists call the *hidden curriculum*, which refers to the idea that there are many educational norms that students are expected to adhere to, but they tend to be left unarticulated and therefore are functionally rendered invisible.

For students who are familiar with the conventions of middle- and upper-class culture, which are often very similar to those of educational settings, the process of adapting to school can be easier because it is closer to what students already know and what seems normal. Because they possess this valuable knowledge, middle- and upper-class students tend to go through school with greater cultural and social capital, which gives them distinct academic advantages, including linguistic advantages (Bourdieu, 1991). Middle- and upper-class students tend to come to school already knowing how to use the standardized English that is valued in educational settings. This prior familiarity and greater "ability to understand and use [the] 'educated' language" that is valued in school gives middle- and upper-class students greater linguistic capital (Sullivan, 2001, p. 893).

Calarco (2011) found, for instance, that elementary school students from middle-class backgrounds are adept at asking for help, using "direct and proactive strategies" that include calling out or approaching the teacher (p. 873). In this study, the teachers tended to respond to these types of requests positively, both by giving extra or immediate help to the middle-class students and by viewing them as motivated and proactive learners. The positive attention, extra help, and higher expectations gave the middle-class students a cumulative advantage over students from working-class backgrounds (Calarco, 2011). Students from middle- and upper-class backgrounds also can have an edge when it comes to testing. Because they possess greater linguistic and cultural capital in school environments, they often already have "a knowledge of the 'rules of the game' of academic assessments" (Sullivan, 2007, para. 3.8). When students possess linguistic and cultural know-how, it not only affects how teachers view these students and form expectations of them but also how the students make choices and form educational expectations and aspirations for themselves (Calarco, 2011). The fact that some students are more advantaged than others, even in the early grades, directly affects their educational achievement, which affects their jobs and other opportunities.

Our framework for approaching differences in linguistic capital draws on a model of privilege, based on McIntosh (1988) and Chen-Hayes, Chen, and Athar (1999). Students who come to school speaking nonstandardized varieties of English or who otherwise speak in ways that do not conform to schools' expectations are often at a disadvantage. In contrast, students who come to school already knowing the norms and conventions of standardized English typically have several advantages. In Figure 3.2, we list seven privileges of standardized English, which speakers carry in "invisible dictionar-

FIGURE 3.2. Seven Privileges of Standardized English

1. Standardized English–speaking students can usually be assured that the newspapers, magazines, books, and other media they encounter at school will be in the type of English they are already familiar with.
2. Standardized English–speaking students can usually be assured that they will not be mocked or teased for how they pronounce their words.
3. Standardized English–speaking students can usually be assured that they will not be thought of as being less intelligent because of how they talk.
4. Standardized English–speaking students can usually be assured that standardized test instructions and materials will be written in the English they are already familiar with.
5. Standardized English–speaking students can usually be assured that most of their educators will communicate with them in the type of English the students are already familiar with.
6. Standardized English–speaking students can generally be assured that the way they talk will not be the subject of jokes or belittling in mainstream TV shows or movies.
7. Standardized English–speaking students can generally be assured that their pronunciation, intonation, and sentence structure will not interfere with their ability to be assessed accurately, to interact with authority figures, or, later in life, to obtain housing and be hired for a job.

ies" (Charity Hudley & Mallinson, 2011). This list of privileges is provided to prompt consideration of how to foster a linguistically inclusive classroom climate. According to Chen-Hayes and colleagues (1999), it is important that educators, students, administrators, parents, staff, and others be aware of and discuss issues of privilege so that everyone can advocate for linguistic respect, diversity, and equality.

Linguistic Stereotypes and Linguistic Prejudice

The message that certain ways of speaking are more valued than others is often woven indirectly into our cultural norms about school and schooling, but it can also be expressed directly and overtly. Language is one of the first things that we notice when we interact with other people and often one of the first things that we judge. As we discussed in Chapter 2, some language varieties are deemed socially prestigious, while others, such as those spoken by many people from working-class backgrounds, people from the South and Appalachia, or by many African Americans, for example, may be devalued—not because of any natural or inherent linguistic deficiency, but because social stigma and bias surrounds certain language forms.

Ideologies about language can translate directly into stereotypes about the people who speak in those ways. Purcell-Gates (1997) conducted a

2-year ethnography of a White Appalachian family and focused on the literacy experiences of a young boy named Donny. Because of their strong Appalachian accents and the fact that the family lived in poverty, Donny and his mother were assumed to be less intelligent. In fact, Donny's 4th-grade teacher described Donny's mother to another teacher by saying, "I knew she was ignorant just as soon as she opened her mouth!" Because of the interaction of linguistic, cultural, and economic differences, Donny was thought to be less capable than other students of achieving in school, which gave him a serious educational disadvantage. Stereotypes can also be activated when listeners judge a speaker on the basis of just an accent, without knowing anything about the speaker's cultural or social class background. The Appalachian author Linda Scott DeRosier (1999) recalled one instance when, after presenting a paper at a scholarly conference, a professor from the audience told her, "I don't think I have ever heard an intelligent person talk the way you do" (p. 67). DeRosier also recounted her visit to the University of Kentucky, where one student from eastern Kentucky said "she was afraid to speak in her other classes, because she was worried that students would make fun of her accent" (Locklear, 2011, p. 94).

Speakers who absorb messages that their use of language is wrong, incorrect, dumb, or stigmatized can experience *linguistic insecurity*, a term coined by linguist William Labov (1972b) to refer to the fact that speakers who internalize negative linguistic messages may feel insecure, anxious, unconfident, or apprehensive when communicating. They may doubt their ability to communicate effectively, may not believe in themselves, and may question their self-worth. Any student can experience linguistic insecurity, although some students may be more sensitive to it than others and may vary in the degree to which they are aware that language can be a basis for judgment and stereotyping. This variability underscores the need for educators to be particularly attuned to situations in which students' linguistic insecurity might affect their academic experiences and performance, consciously or subconsciously.

Linguistic Microaggressions

Negative messages about language can be experienced as *linguistic microaggressions*. The term *microaggressions* refers to everyday biases and indignities faced by members of marginalized groups (Sue, 2010). Racial, gender, and sexual-orientation microaggressions are typically discussed in academic contexts, but the concept also applies to language. For instance, the statement "I've never heard an intelligent person talk the way you do" is a common linguistic microaggression. It suggests that the person whose accent is being remarked upon isn't smart and implies that other people who

BOX 3.3. A SOCIOLINGUIST'S VIGNETTE: Teaching About the Link Between Language and Culture

Dr. Catherine Evans Davies, Professor of Linguistics and Chair of the Department of English at the University of Alabama

I grew up in the New York City area, the child of upwardly aspiring middle-class parents from Wilkes-Barre, Pennsylvania. My father spent a decade as a high school English teacher, and I suspect that my negative impressions of Northeastern vernaculars came from his influence. At home, I mastered a dialect that was what the school wanted, so I never had any difficulty in American schools related to the dialect that I spoke; in fact, I never really learned how to revise my written essays because I was able to produce an acceptable product at the last minute using my native dialect.

It was only when I had an extraordinary experience during my high school years that I came up against prejudice against my dialect. My father, by now a professor of educational administration at Teachers College, had received a Ford Foundation grant to study school administration in Europe. Taking an innovative ethnographic approach, he rejected a quick tour of a lot of schools and insisted upon month-long residences in schools in England, France, and Germany, with his children enrolled in the schools for firsthand experience. It was because of this study that I found myself in a German Gymnasium (an elite academic high school) for a month in the vicinity of Frankfurt in West Germany. In addition to studying Greek and Latin, the students were studying English, with weekly classes taught by a woman of Scottish descent. Just after I arrived I was invited to make a presentation to the class, and I talked about my American school and my life in the United States. It wasn't immediately obvious to me, because I was so caught up in the linguistic and cultural shock of trying to cope in this environment with one semester of high school German, that there were no more English classes during the next several weeks of my stay. When I was about to leave, a group of girls who had befriended me got me in a room in one of their homes and said that there was something that they needed to tell me because I was their friend: After I made my presentation at that first English class, they had been told that the English classes would be suspended because they didn't want the students to imitate my "terrible American accent." They, of course, liked the way I sounded and wanted to learn how to swear in American English.

This was my first experience of discrimination on the basis of accent. When I came to the American South, to Alabama, I brought with me this personal experience. I also brought an awareness of my own prejudice against Northeastern vernaculars, but at the same time the realization that I didn't have an ingrained prejudice against Southern vernaculars. It occurred to me that I might be a good teacher in this environment, because I didn't have that prejudice. I was in a position to appreciate Southern vernacular in all of its richness and potentially to project appreciation to my Southern students.

Tuscaloosa, Alabama, where the University of Alabama campus is located, has become associated, through football publicity, with the local ribs restaurant

Dreamland, which was founded by an African American family. This restaurant was established in 1958 by Jim "Big Daddy" Bishop, whose image still appears on the logo. The Dreamland Bar-B-Que ribs are eaten with the hands and served with a side of Wonder Bread. The well-known slogan used in Dreamland advertising on billboards around town is: "Ain't nothing like 'em nowhere!"

I regularly teach an upper-division undergraduate course on dialectology in the English Department at the University of Alabama. It is an interesting challenge to teach about language variation in a region where a stigmatized variety is spoken, especially with many students who have achieved admission to the state's most prestigious public university by modifying their dialects. Many, especially those from rural backgrounds, report that they speak Southern vernacular at home (and would be judged to be "putting on airs" if they didn't) but then shift to a more standardized English at the university, especially for written assignments. A grammatical pattern that many don't recognize as part of Southern American dialect until they try to write it in a university context is the double modal construction (as in, *might could*). Many students are ambivalent about their regional dialect, having internalized the negative stereotypes so prevalent in American society. One challenge I face, as a native New Yorker who spent many years in California before coming to Alabama, is to show students that I understand and respect Southern American English; my goal, of course, is to develop understanding and appreciation of its unique patterning and to help students to set aside their own prescriptive attitudes at the same time that I help them to develop their own command of standardized English.

At the appropriate point in the semester, when I judge that the students are ready to suspend prescriptivism enough to entertain wider communicative possibilities, I ask them to consider the Dreamland Bar-B-Que slogan: "Ain't nothing like 'em nowhere!" We might start simply by considering the *'em* and noting that attempt to capture spoken language by using an apostrophe to stand for the voiced interdental fricative sound represented by the letters *th* in *them*. Then we might go on to wonder why the slogan doesn't drop the *g* in *nothing* by substituting an apostrophe, since surely a person who said *'em* would also say *nothin'*. Next I ask the students to consider *ain't* and its status as *the* stigmatized form in English for several centuries now, even though it happily survives in the vernacular. We consider who is speaking in the slogan and who the audience is for the advertising. Then we move to the double and triple negative, and I ask them what communicative effect is achieved by this doubling and tripling of negation. If the class is open enough to seeing the communicative possibilities of nonstandardized varieties, then instead of a response like, "Well, you can't have double or triple negatives in proper English," a student will say something like, "It creates increasing emphasis for the slogan!" My favorite response to the slogan—incorporating not only a translation but also the essence of the link between language and culture—was from a White male Alabamian undergraduate, who said, "Would *you* want to eat ribs cooked by somebody who said [and he then produced this utterance while imitating a non-Southern accent]: 'There is nothing like them anywhere'"?

speak with that accent aren't smart either. Another linguistic microaggression, which tends to be made toward people of color, is the statement "You talk White" or "You sound White," although the statement "You sound Black" (or "Mexican," "Indian," etc.) can also sometimes be made. These microaggressions can imply that members of racial or ethnic groups are expected to talk and "sound" the same, that anyone who doesn't is deviant, and that some cultures are not worth identifying with. Furthermore, it can imply that the speaker in question, because of how she or he talks, no longer belongs to or identifies with her or his home culture, which may not be true. Other linguistic microaggressions can be made on the basis of gender ("You sound like a girl"), sexuality ("You sound gay"), social class ("You sound like a snob"), region of origin ("You sound like a hillbilly"), and many other social characteristics.

Pierce (1974) conceived of microaggressions as "mini-assaults," because they are subtle and may be invisible to others (p. 516). In fact, perpetrators may not realize that they have delivered a snub, a slight, or an insult to the recipients. According to Sue (2010), microaggressions are commonplace, constant, and continuing experiences for members of marginalized groups in our society. Even though they may occur in brief exchanges, microaggressions can result in serious psychological and social consequences—such as feelings of powerlessness, a sense of inferiority, and pressure to assimilate—that can have a damaging cumulative effect (Sue, 2010).

Microaggressions are often not thought to be a big deal by those who aren't affected by them, and sometimes they can even be framed as or intended to be compliments. As DeRosier recalled about the professor who said he had never heard someone intelligent who talked the way she did, "he thought he was paying me a compliment" (1999, p. 67). The Microaggressions Project (2010–2013) provides an online forum where individuals can anonymously post their own experiences with microaggressions. One post stated:

> "Wow. You speak so quickly and you enunciate your words so well!" [Those were] the first words out of the mouth of a white man in Washington, DC, after my mother gave a presentation. My mother has a very strong Southern accent. It made her feel completely belittled, and like she couldn't be taken seriously in the professional world. (July 23, 2011)

Another post from March 2, 2011, told a similar story: "I'm so impressed —I can't hear any accent when you talk! Client (white, mid 50s), to me (Hispanic, mid 20s)." A post by an African American student described being asked by a professor, "Where did you go to school to write like this?

[Because] you say 'ask' versus 'ax' and your writing is impeccable" (May 2, 2012). We have heard stories from African American educators of other similar microaggressions, including "You have such an interesting name!" and "I didn't expect for you to sound so eloquent."

A similar backhanded compliment, "You're so articulate," is a linguistic microaggression that many African Americans have experienced. As Alim and Smitherman (2012) explained, "'compliments' like 'articulate' and 'speaks so well' are too often racially coded to mean 'articulate . . . for a black person'" (p. 35). In other words, these "compliments" suggest that the speaker is expecting African Americans to sound and behave inarticulately and therefore is surprised when they don't. Alim and Smitherman pointed out that their analysis applies to groups other than African Americans: "*articulate* is used by members of the dominant culture to describe the speech of those on the social and linguistic margins, such as children, southerners, immigrants, second language learners, and so on" (2012, p. 50). Linguistic microaggressions can therefore interact with microaggressions based on ethnicity, gender, sexual orientation, age, region of origin, and more.

Linguistic microaggressions can also occur when certain individuals are expected or asked to speak on behalf of members of a group that they belong to or are assumed to belong to. For instance, a linguistic microaggression may occur when an African American student is assigned to read aloud a piece of dialogue written by a Black author because it is assumed that the student will be able to "naturally" represent the author's voice. A similar example, from a student in a post on the Microaggressions Project online forum, stated: "'I'm sure you can speak to this.'—Teacher, referring to me in a class discussing how race influences therapy. I'm the only Black person in the room" (January 14, 2012). Situations in which individuals feel that they are being asked to speak as a token member or as a spokesperson for their assumed group can cause embarrassment, pressure to "get it right," anxiety, shame, or feelings of being the subject of unwanted attention. Palmer (2012) recounted his experience in a college classroom when, on Columbus Day, a professor pointed at a student who looked to be Native American (though he had not self-identified as such) and said, "You. You're Native right? What is the Native American perspective on Christopher Columbus?" As he watched the student struggle to respond, Palmer realized, "Asking a student to speak on behalf of their social group (be it race, class, gender, etc.) is akin to saying 'you people are all the same.'" Palmer decided that when he became a teacher one day, he would let his students "decide when and where they want the spotlight put on them." Linguistic and cultural awareness can help avoid such situations, even inadvertent ones, in which students experience linguistic and cultural microaggressions.

BOX 3.4. FOR LINGUISTIC REFLECTION: Linguistic Microaggressions

Language plays a significant role in the classroom, particularly in situations such as discussion time and in-class presentations. The following questions help educators consider the linguistic and cultural climate of educational settings and interactions.

- Are assumptions made about some students' cultural backgrounds or academic abilities that influence when/how these students are called upon or what they are expected to talk about?
- When certain students are presenting in front of the class, do other students make comments about their language? Are some students routinely praised, while others typically receive negative feedback?
- With regard to classroom assessment and discipline, are clear expectations communicated to students regarding the use of language? Is the way that some students communicate viewed as being hostile or aggressive? Is there consistency with respect to which verbal infractions lead to disciplinary action?

It can sometimes be difficult for educators to make these sorts of assessments about their own classrooms. Personal introspection combined with talking about these issues with other educators, whether via one-on-one conversations or in small groups, can help reveal the role of language and culture in classroom and school contexts.

Names and Labels

What we call ourselves and what other people call us are integral to how we self-identify and how we identify others. Yet, names and labels can be at the center of linguistic stereotypes and linguistic prejudice, whether through microaggressions or more overt offenses. There is a long history of linguistic abuses perpetrated against Native American students, who were expected to use English and were often forbidden to use their native languages. Sometimes students were even forced to change their names. In his memoir, Dakota Indian Luther Standing Bear explained that, when he was in school, students had to choose from a list of English names on the chalkboard. "When my turn came," he said, "I took the pointer and acted as if I were about to touch an enemy" (1928, p. 137).

Names and labels include terms for self-reference—terms that people use to define themselves—which are often debated and in flux. Baugh (1999) found generational differences in African Americans' attitudes toward the terms *colored* and *Negro*. Over 80% of respondents under age 35 found both terms disrespectful, but only about 30% of respondents over age 50 felt the same, because they had grown up in the 1960s when *colored* and *Negro* were more commonly used. The terms *Black*, *person of color*, and *African American* are also complex and changing. Burch (2012) described Gibré George, a man in his 30s who set up a Facebook page called "Don't Call Me African American." In an interview, George said, "I prefer to be called American, but if you must further define me, then use the term black or person of color. The term African American just doesn't settle right in my stomach because it's not accurate"—he meant that the term fails to capture his full background, which includes Caribbean roots. Scholars have found that many Black people now view the term *African American* as too specific to account for their diverse origins. Anne, who was interviewed for Burch's article, explained, "The larger issue is that, over the years, people of the African diaspora lost the right to name themselves. It's not really about what is right or wrong but how people see and think of themselves, which is a personal choice."

The debate over names and naming traditions is not only about collective naming, but also about individual names. Lieberson and Mikelson (1995) analyzed the innovative naming practices among African American parents. In their study, African Americans were more likely than White parents to give their children unique names, a practice that dates back to the 1960s, when many African Americans "were stressing their distinctive culture and turned to their African roots" (p. 940). Sometimes unique names are created through spelling variation (e.g., Derrius, Jasmyne) or by combining popular sets of sounds and syllables (e.g., Jabar, Lanique). They may be adapted from existing words, such as geographical names (e.g., Affrica, D'Asia) or names of products (e.g., Chanel, Bentley). Inspiration for unique names can be drawn from African names (e.g., Kwame, a name common among the Akan and Twi peoples of Ghana), the names of prominent African American political or cultural leaders (e.g., Barack, Aretha), and combining the names of parents or other relatives (e.g., Darneisha, from Darnell and Keisha).

Unique African American names are often mocked, however. In a post on the Microaggressions Project online forum, one individual reported having heard the following statement: "Can't wait to show all my friends my ghetto-fabulous ride. She needs a name . . . something ethnic . . . Laquisha?" (January 20, 2012). This statement reflects the stereotype that unique African American names are a marker of lower-class status. Unique African American names can be cast more subtly as being "different" or "unpronounceable" in ways that send a problematic cultural message. In February 2013, Quvenzhané Wallis, the youngest-ever nominee for the Academy

Award for Best Actress, was referred to by White interviewers as "Little Q" and as "Annie" rather than by her actual name. As Clayton (2013) pointed out, "refusing to learn how to pronounce Quvenzhané's name says, pointedly . . . 'I am going to call you what I want to call you in spite of what you call yourself,'" which carries an underlying message of power and control. Countering messages of assimilation, Kenyan-born Somali poet and writer Warsan Shire (2011) wrote, "Give your daughters difficult names. Give your daughters names that command the full use of tongue. My name makes you want to tell me the truth. My name doesn't allow me to trust anyone that cannot pronounce it right."

The ways that African American–sounding names are mocked and stereotyped can translate into racial biases and have measurably detrimental effects. In their article, "Are Emily and Greg More Employable than Lakisha and Jamal?", Bertrand and Mullainathan (2004) responded to help-wanted ads in Boston and Chicago newspapers with fictitious resumes, half of which had uniquely African American–sounding names and half of which had White-sounding names. The White-sounding names received 50% more callbacks for interviews, a gap consistent across occupation, industry, and employer size. Research has found similar biases against foreign-sounding names (Arai & Thoursie, 2009).

The question of how educators and students respond to the names and labels that students use to refer to themselves and others is of critical importance in classrooms and schools. Names and labels are strongly tied to personal and family identity and cultural traditions, as well as to social and historical context, and students, parents, and educators may be sensitive when they feel that negative attitudes are being expressed toward their names. It is particularly important for educators to be aware of the role of names and labels in the larger problem of linguistic bullying.

Bullying and Slurs

Bullying, a behavior that can be verbal as well as physical, is a challenge in many classrooms and schools. In a recent study of school bullying that surveyed over 7,000 U.S. adolescents, Wang, Iannotti, and Nansel (2009) found that more than 53% of students had been verbally bullied at school at least once in the past 2 months. Linguistic bullying can occur when students call each other names or use unwelcome nicknames. It can also manifest in the use of slurs and insults.

Slurs that are based on race or ethnicity can be seen as a linguistic manifestation of prejudice and discrimination. It is often difficult to define slurs, however, because what is a slur to some is not necessarily a slur to others (Henderson, 2003). Because communication is influenced by history, society, culture, and identity—our first linguistic truth—the same word used as a slur in one context can sometimes be used in a different context, often by in-group members, in ways that are not intended to be derogatory (for instance, as an ethnic label or an identity marker). Two ethnic labels/slurs that are often hotly contested and complicated in their use are *redneck* and *nigger*. Our discussion of these terms can be used as a model for how educators can consider other controversial labels/slurs—including *gay*, *fag*, *retard/retarded*, *ghetto*, and *bitch*—that may be encountered at school.

The term *redneck* has many definitions. According to Reed (1986) and Hartigan (2003), a redneck is often thought to be a person who is ignorant, uneducated, or intellectually limited; who is from a lower social class; and who is prejudiced or racist. Rednecks are also frequently thought of as lazy in actions, thoughts, and speech, and these perceptions are linked to common views of Southern English speech as slow and incorrect (Charity Hudley & Mallinson, 2011). Many speakers in the contemporary United States use the term *redneck* in ways that echo these definitions. For example, when Christine conducted field research in western North Carolina with her colleague Becky Childs, they interviewed a group of three adolescents—one White, the others African American—who used the term *redneck* to refer to Whites they viewed as racist (Childs & Mallinson, 2006). But this definition for *redneck* was not the only one that speakers in this community used. One young man, whom we called Roger, was in his late 20s and self-identified as Black. He routinely referred to himself as a redneck, even calling himself "the biggest redneck" in his community during one interview. Similarly, Roger's sister, who was in her early 30s, used the term *redneck* in a nonderogatory way to refer to men who enjoyed hunting and who were "country." Unlike the adolescents from this community, who used the term *redneck* specifically to refer to Whites, Roger and his sister did not use it to indicate a person's racial or ethnic background. Even within this small community, the term *redneck* was used in two competing ways: first, as a slur that highlighted social divisions and boundaries based on race, and second, as a nonracial label that marked regional and local identity (Childs & Mallinson, 2006). As this example illustrates, ethnic labels, like all words, are dynamic and variable with respect to who uses them, how they are used, and what they mean.

The term *nigger* is similarly complex and occupies a unique place in the English language. As noted by Henderson (2003), despite the fact that this term is used in literary works, "it now ranks as perhaps the most offensive and inflammatory racial slur in English" (p. 65). In fact, the term is considered so taboo and offensive that it is often referred to by a euphemism, *the n-word*. Much like the term *redneck*, the n-word has a multifarious history as a racial slur, an ethnic label, and an identity marker, and its use is

BOX 3.5. CURRICULAR CONNECTIONS: Debating the N-Word

In a vignette published in *Teaching Tolerance*, Carrie Craven (2011), a middle school English teacher in Louisiana, described an assignment in which students created their own dictionaries. When one student asked whether they were allowed to include the word *nigga*, she responded, "I'm not sure how I feel about that. What do you think?" Craven explained that her goal for this project was to involve students in a debate about the power of words. As classroom discussion unfolded, some students thought the word was "just what we call each other," while others viewed it as a relic of slavery. Ultimately, through "exploring the history and implications and *power* of specific words," Craven explained, her students started to "understand that every time you use a word it essentially has two meanings: (1.) What you meant by it, and (2.) What it means to the person who hears it." As Craven's example illustrates, having a conversation about words, meaning, and usage is the first step in fostering healthy debate about critical issues of language and culture.

debated "furiously within the African American community as it is across all American communities" (Henderson, 2003, p. 65). While many African Americans find the term *nigger* reprehensible and refuse to use it, research has found that African Americans under the age of 30 are likely to use the modified terms *nigga* or *niggah* in ways that they feel are amiable or neutral (Alim & Smitherman, 2012; Asim, 2007; Henderson, 2003; Kennedy, 2002). In his book, *The N Word: Who Can Say It, Who Shouldn't, and Why*, Asim (2007) reviewed 400 years of usage of the term *nigger* and argued that this word, more than any other in the English language, embodies racial oppression; even though it has taken on new meaning and usage in the contemporary era, it is still fraught with tension. Rather than banning the word, Asim suggested, deep critical thought is fundamentally necessary for speakers to be able to make informed choices about their language and the words they use.

For many students, racial slurs are unfortunately not a thing of the past but rather something they routinely encounter. Dickter and Newton (2013) conducted a study in which 47 college students recorded all prejudicial comments they heard for one week. Participants reported that they had heard an average of almost nine racist comments over the course of the week, including comments in which the n-word was used, with male students hearing and making around twice as many racist comments as female students. At the same time, students also often used the n-word or variations on it, such as *nigga*, in ways that were not intended to be derogatory.

Given the fact that emotions run high when the n-word is involved and that its usage and meaning vary across speakers and generations, thoughtful discussion is needed when students and educators encounter the word. In

Box 3.6, a high school English teacher who has worked with us described the importance of having honest conversations with different groups at his school when he was asked by students to lead a project on the n-word. (In Chapter 4, we continue our discussion of the n-word in literature and present a second vignette from this educator in Box 4.8 on pp. 96–97, in which he explains the academic details of this project.)

BOX 3.6. AN EDUCATOR'S VIGNETTE: Studying the N-Word: Beginning the Conversation

Cleveland Winfield,
10th-Grade English and Hip-Hop Verse & Poetry Teacher

During the fall of 2006, through a series of discussions with my 10th-grade English students, I discovered that two of my gifted and talented pupils were very inquisitive and daring: They wanted to conduct an in-depth analysis of the n-word. In this vignette, I explain how I began the conversation about this project with my students, my principal, other teachers, parents, and the community.

Once my students and I agreed that we wanted to pursue a project on the n-word, I gathered some feedback from the students as to why they wanted to engage in this project and began designing the curriculum. I then informed our principal about this gifted and talented project. He had some reservations about our desire to bring this study into a classroom. He was insistent that we have to remember that we live in a small Southern town, and we have to acknowledge the feelings that can be conjured up when this explosive word is said or heard in any context; he wanted to avoid any possible racial tension. As a compromise, he approved my proposal to explore the study of the n-word within the context of a gifted and talented project that occurred outside of the academic school day.

I conducted this gifted and talented project for 2 years, after which I began to teach a new elective, "Cultural Perspectives," at my high school and for a local community college's Upward Bound program, which enabled me to take the study of the n-word directly to a wider demographic of the student population. At the end of the course, for the Upward Bound summer session awards ceremony, the students and I gave a public presentation about our Cultural Perspectives class that highlighted our exploration of the n-word. I composed the following paragraphs in hopes of providing the students, parents, and educators with a respectfully thoughtful introduction to our presentation. I knew this was necessary to do, given the history of that explosive slur, the fact that we live in the South, the wide array of perspectives and strong emotions that stem from the usage of that word, and the reality that racial tensions still exist in our community, as well as in the country at large. It is my hope that this introduction may serve as some sort of guide/model for teachers who desire to teach the n-word or some other controversial term/issue.

"From our first steps to degradation on this stolen land, to the infamous lynching of the Ku Klux Klan, and on to the daring comedic sketches of Chris Rock and Dave Chappelle, the 'n-word' has been, and perhaps always will be, a troublesome expression that generates an array of reactions from blacks of all ages, as well as scrutiny and confusion from people of all ethnicities around the world. Through a variety of genres or educational mediums such as response writing prompts, poems, song lyrics, discussion questions, and comedy sketches, my students and I have addressed some serious societal and cultural issues. Predominantly focused on the study of the 'n-word,' Cultural Perspectives has challenged our students to view and understand their stances and beliefs and the stances and beliefs of those that they may oppose.

The following student presentation will include some direct references to the actual 'n-word.' In other words, rather than merely reciting the euphemism, you will hear a few students say 'nigger' as they share their presentation here tonight at the awards ceremony. These students will use this derogatory term in an educational context. It is not their intent to offend anyone in the audience with their recitation or usage of this poisonous slur. Instead, it is their hope that they will shed some light on the various definitions, usages, and/or interpretations of this troublesome word. The Cultural Perspectives course has allowed our students to begin to do just that. Once again, it is not our intent to offend anyone in the audience with our usage of 'nigger' in our presentations, and we apologize if you are bothered by our decision to do so. We truly believe that we need to face this troublesome expression head-on and that we need to provide some educational insight on the various definitions, usages, spin-off phrases, and/or interpretations of a word that has plagued the English language, and perhaps more importantly humanity, for the past four centuries."

SPEAKING UP AND SPEAKING OUT: LINGUISTIC AGENCY

Linguistic and cultural issues—including communicative burdens, microaggressions, bullying, and slurs—can deeply affect those who speak nonstandardized varieties of English. In this section, we explore how people who experience these situations might react. When speakers use language to accomplish social action, we can think of them as asserting their *linguistic agency* (Ahern, 2001). In the face of linguistic prejudice, some speakers may respond by asserting their linguistic agency more directly and overtly, whereas others may respond more indirectly or subtly.

Some speakers who internalize the message that others view their language as wrong or backward may assert their linguistic agency by striving to speak so "perfectly" that they engage in *hypercorrection*. According to Wolfram and Schilling-Estes (2006), when speakers feel a need to use extremely standard or "correct" language, they may extend a language form beyond its regular linguistic boundaries. In other words, some speakers are so concerned with getting their grammar or pronunciation "right" that they overarticulate in ways that miss the standardized target they are trying to emulate (for instance, consider the phrase "between you and I," a hypercorrection of the standardized form "between you and me"). Linguists have found that lower-middle-class and upper-working-class speakers often hypercorrect, perhaps because they are concerned with raising their socioeconomic status to the next higher level. The use of hypercorrect language has also been found to be more characteristic of women (Lakoff, 1975), particularly Black women (Morgan, 2004). As Locklear (2011) pointed out, literacy and literacy practices are often closely associated with women. It therefore makes sense that women and girls may experience more identity-based dilemmas about language than men and boys do, particularly in high stakes settings such as in school and at work.

Speakers who face microaggressions, prejudice, and discrimination may also react with internalization, a process whereby members of stigmatized groups accept negative messages about their self-worth. Steele and Aronson (1995) analyzed *stereotype threat*, a concept that refers to the fact that negative social stereotypes and lower expectations can severely affect test takers from stigmatized groups on a psychological level. For example, conventional testing situations that include a verbal component have been shown to cause African American students to become hesitant and taciturn (Labov, 1972a) or to perform less well than their ability level would predict (Steele & Aronson, 1995). Stereotype threat can also operate in the classroom, where students from stigmatized groups may avoid speaking up in class out of the fear that if they make a mistake it will confirm negative stereotypes about them in other students' or educators' minds. For example, residents of Appalachia have been known to not discuss challenges related to school or educational attainment with outsiders, out of fear that "doing so would only further bolster pervasive stereotypes that cast the region as illiterate, notions residents understandably want to avoid" (Locklear, 2011, p. 3). Students can also be sensitive to situations in which members of their race or gender are underrepresented, and therefore they are one of very few or the sole representative of their social group—a situation known as solo status (Sekaquaptewa & Thompson, 2002). These situations can often cause writing and speaking anxiety and thereby directly affect how students behave and talk in class. In fact, Steele (2003) found that "the most achievement oriented students, who were also the most skilled, motivated, and confident, were the most impaired by stereotype threat" (p. 120). Thus, even exceptional students faced with this situation may hold diminished educational expectations for themselves.

Students may also choose to not speak up in school because there is a disparity between the language they are comfortable using and the language they are expected to use. Verdi and Ebsworth (2009) reported the story of Terese, who explained, "I know there were instances when I thought I wasn't smart enough to speak. . . . I realized that at home I was being told not to speak like the other children, but when I went to school, I was told that the English my grandmother taught me wasn't correct . . . I was silenced; I didn't talk in school" (p. 191). These situations have been found to particularly affect girls (Delpit & Dowdy, 2008). Silence is an all too common mode of expression for girls, who often have a sense of fear about sounding "stupid" or "wrong," as well as for all students who have internalized a sense of shame about how they communicate. Secondary English educators likely have had the experience of trying to reach out to the shy or silent student who never speaks up in class even though her or his insights would be valued. Because the secondary English classroom is often a place where discussions about words and communication are held and where the use of language is critically examined, secondary English educators are well suited to have conversations about linguistic ideologies, attitudes, stereotypes, and prejudice, as well as students' responses to these circumstances—which can include silence. By having these conversations, educators and students can seek to understand and overcome linguistic challenges in ways that foster positive student engagement and confident self-expression.

In response to microaggressions, prejudice, and discrimination, some speakers might assert their linguistic agency by speaking out. As writer and poet Audre Lorde (1984) put it, there is a need to end the "tyrannies of silence." By "shar[ing] a commitment to language and to the power of language, and to the reclaiming of that language which has been made to work against us," Lorde said, we can transform silence into language and action (pp. 41–43). The author bell hooks, a Black woman who left Kentucky to attend Stanford University, echoed Lorde's sentiments when she stated, "Moving from silence into speech is for the oppressed, the colonized, the exploited. . . . It is the act of speech . . . that is the expression of our movement from object to subject—the liberated voice" (hooks, 1989, p. 9). According to Lorde and hooks, by speaking out, diverse voices are added to the conversation in ways that counteract silencing.

Secondary English educators can foster students' linguistic agency and counteract silencing by discussing effective and appropriate models for speaking out and speaking up at school. In *Teaching Tolerance* (n.d.a), the activity "How to Implement 'Speak Up at School'" is designed to help educators and students create a safe school climate. Educators are asked to read a statement on how to create a welcoming school environment and then to consider four statements: (1) Name examples of biased language you hear at your school. (2) What words have become colloquial yet are still harmful, biased language? (3) Do your students understand intent vs. impact? (4) What are you currently doing or what have you done in the past to establish a safe environment where all students can learn? Educators can consider how to prepare themselves and their students to speak up by using basic linguistic strategies, such as "That word is hurtful." In short online videos that accompany this *Teaching Tolerance* activity, educators discuss real-life challenges in which they were confronted with the question of whether or not—and how—to speak up. *Teaching Tolerance* (n.d.b) also provides kits and a downloadable handbook, *Speak Up!*, free to educators.

Speakers can also assert their linguistic agency more subtly, but still powerfully, by using their own authentic language. Particularly within safe cultural spaces, where speakers may be free from linguistic stereotypes and microaggressions, authentic language can have powerful symbolic and communicative value. For members of linguistically marginalized groups, the use of nonstandardized varieties of English can signal in-group status and convey solidarity. For example, the Appalachian author Linda Scott DeRosier described how her father resisted speaking in standardized English, because he preferred to use his home variety of Appalachian English. As she explained, her father would often say, "'[Eastern Kentucky] is the prettiest place they is.' And that's the way he said it, too, using 'they' for 'there,' though he knew the difference" (Locklear, 2011, p. 103). Like her father, DeRosier maintains her Appalachian accent in her speech, and she uses Appalachian linguistic features in her writing. Many individuals choose to express themselves in the nonstandardized varieties of English that they learned and were surrounded by in their communities of origin. While their linguistic choices may startle or surprise some listeners, they may also prompt listeners to question stereotypes and realign their beliefs about language and culture. The use of nonstandardized varieties of English can thus help marginalized speakers resist the pressure of mainstream norms, assert their identities, and confront social stigma and subjugation.

Classrooms can be an excellent place to discuss with students the concept linguistic agency, particularly in the face of linguistic stereotypes, prejudice, and microaggressions, and particularly as a way to mitigate fear. In *Teaching Tolerance*, Madrid-Campbell and Hughes (n.d.) created an article for grades 9–12 on the topic of *linguicism*, a term coined by linguist Tove Skutnabb-Kangas (1988) to refer to discrimination and the reproduction of unequal power dynamics based on language. In a series of exercises, Madrid-Campbell and Hughes invite students to think about their language attitudes, derive their own definition of linguicism, and create a skit to combat it. Similarly, in the *Teaching Tolerance* article "Everyone Has an Accent," Wolfram (2000) asked students and educators to consider what it means when someone says that another person "talks funny." He discussed "truth and fiction about dialects" and explained how our language attitudes are tied to not only our perceptions of language but also to our perceptions of people.

We can also discuss with students how we acquire and derive our beliefs and attitudes about language. Do we learn them from the media? In school? In our neighborhoods and communities? From our peers and family members? Some questions that educators can pose to students as food

BOX 3.7. AN EDUCATOR'S VIGNETTE: A Dialect as Diversity Literature Unit

Ashleigh Greene Wade,
Upper School English and History Teacher

I have to admit I was nervous about teaching a literature unit on dialect and language variations. As someone who has spent a great deal of my life hiding or being ashamed of my accent in one way or another, I did not want to deliver the unit in a way that would perpetuate stereotypes or enforce negative notions about different groups of people. I wanted to create a safe and honest environment.

I opened my discussion of language variation by introducing dialect as a literary term. I let my students listen to sound clips of people from various geographical regions within the United States and see if they could identify the speakers' origins based on linguistic features. The students enjoyed this activity, and some of them were able to recognize patterns that their own family members use.

Before getting into an in-depth discussion of language variation, many students asked why a person would try to minimize his or her accent or change his or her voice. I allowed these questions to lead into an explanation of standardized English and stigmas that might be associated with nonstandardized varieties. During our conversation, one student asked if having an accent makes a person's English wrong or improper, so we had a discussion about language variations and how these variations represent diverse forms of English rather than substandard or improper forms. Students were eager to talk about their own experiences, and several mentioned that they don't like being called Southern or having people point out their Southern accents. We talked about why those feelings exist and the negative stereotypes that have been generated about Southerners. I discussed with my students the fact that Southern English and Southern identities are not substandard and that we should celebrate diverse forms of language and expression.

Once students finished the dialect unit, I had them complete an anonymous survey to tell me what they think they had learned from the unit.

- Students reported learning that, no matter what type of dialect you have, you can still be as important, smart, or equal as anyone else.
- Students learned that they shouldn't judge or make assumptions based on how a person speaks.
- Students gained an appreciation for the idea that there is no right or wrong way to talk. Sometimes speakers may need to use appropriate words and tone in different situations, but they don't need to change the way they talk.

I will definitely be teaching this unit again in the future.

for thought, as classroom discussion starters, or as essay prompts include: What might we assume just from the sound of a person's voice? Are our ideas about language ever the basis for snap judgments that we make about people? From what sources do we get our ideas about language? How can we determine whether they are accurate? How do films and TV shows portray different social attributes through a character's voice? What sorts of accents are used to indicate that a character is smart or not smart? Friendly or not friendly? A villain or a hero? A princess or a queen? A prince or a king? When we encounter stereotypes and potential bias, what can we each do to speak up? These sorts of questions build students' critical language awareness and encourage students to explore how they can counteract negative messages about language and honor diverse forms of expression in their own lives.

CONCLUSION

Our society is rich in linguistic and cultural diversity. Without an understanding of the ways in which culture and language are intertwined, interact, and reflect each other, communication challenges and breakdowns can occur. The challenge in classrooms and schools is often how to begin conversations about issues of culture clashes and miscommunication in a culturally and linguistically responsive manner. As Singleton and Linton (2005) pointed out, sometimes "courageous conversations" about ethnicity, culture, language, and identity require overcoming fear—fear that we will appear ignorant, that we will seem naïve, that we might offend another person, or that we may make a mistake when we engage in conversations about a culture different from our own. According to Tatum (2007), it is important to overcome fear and talk across lines of difference, because communication can open doors:

> In order for there to be meaningful dialogue, fear, whether of anger or isolation, must eventually give way to risk and trust. A leap of faith must be made. It is not easy, and it requires being willing to push past one's fear. [As one of my students once wrote], "At times it feels too risky . . . but I think if people remain equally committed, it can get easier. It's a very stressful process, but I think the consequences of not exploring racial issues are ultimately far more damaging. . . ." (p. 150)

It is important for educators, particularly secondary English educators, to advocate for fostering thoughtful discussion and dialogue about language and culture. Secondary English educators who are informed about language, culture, and identity are better equipped to honor the cultural and linguistic diversity of their students and colleagues. They are also better able to understand the different forms of linguistic capital that students bring with them to the classroom and to understand how and where language variation surfaces in the speaking, reading, and writing of students and in the voices of authors whose texts are taught in secondary English curricula. When a framework of culturally and linguistically responsive pedagogy has been established, authentic dialogue is encouraged and accepted, and diverse voices are valued. Beginning from this place of respect helps establish a strong foundation for student engagement and, as a result, student success.

In Box 3.8, a final vignette introduces the concept (which we build upon in Chapter 4) that literature is a powerful means for educators to encourage all students to let their voices be heard. In this vignette, the author tied a poem from the Harlem Renaissance called "Incident," written by Countee Cullen in 1925, to her own hurtful and harmful experience encountering the n-word at school, 67 years later. With this vignette in mind, in Chapter 4 we examine how language variation in literature can allow authors and readers to express their identities and can be a conduit for important and sometimes challenging cultural conversations.

BOX 3.8. AN EDUCATOR'S VIGNETTE: Finding My Voice

Ruth Harper,
Middle School History Teacher

"Incident," Countee Cullen (1925)

Once riding in old Baltimore,
Heart-filled, head-filled with glee,
I saw a Baltimorean
Keep looking straight at me.
Now I was eight and very small,
And he was no whit bigger,
And so I smiled, but he poked out
His tongue, and called me, "Nigger."
I saw the whole of Baltimore
From May until December;
Of all the things that happened there
That's all that I remember.

I have shared this poem out loud from Harlem Renaissance writer Countee Cullen twice at my school—the school that I attended as a girl, where I also now teach.

I first shared this poem for an assignment when my wonderful freshman English teacher asked us to go out and find a poem that spoke to us. I pored over poetry anthologies until I came across this one from Cullen, a Southern-born, New York City–raised literature nut who attended a rigorous, predominantly White high school in the 1920s. The poet in this piece was "being authentic," and I chose his poem because I felt his words spoke for me at a time when I did not yet feel empowered to speak for myself.

It was in the unusual heat of fall 1992, in a fierce presidential campaign process much like ones we have recently faced, that all of the high school students filed into the old gym for a mock presidential debate. Students in a history class had prepared arguments for each of the three frontrunners and would debate the issues for the school, followed by a mock vote.

Before the debate got started, someone, somewhere in the crowd got the idea to start a note. The notebook paper was passed around and around, and people wrote disparaging remarks about the candidates—some wrote about Republicans and Democrats in general; others wrote "Susie was here" and other silly things. But one thing stood out to me when the note arrived in my hands: Someone had written on the paper in bold letters, "Niggers Suck."

I had been at the school since kindergarten, and no one had ever used that ugly term in my presence, directly or indirectly. I wish that I had been one of those girls who had thicker skin, more like the woman I am now if confronted with the same words, but I wasn't. When I saw that note it completely deflated me. I couldn't even speak. Another African American student sitting next to me took the note to the dean of students before the debate began.

The racial slur written on "the note" was the talk of the school. My skin burned at the thought of it all. How could someone try to reduce my heritage to such a low level with his or her words? Why didn't any of my classmates take the note out of circulation before it made so many rounds around the assembly? Unsatisfied at the thought that this incident should just go away, I decided to investigate myself. My investigation was short-lived. The very first two classmates I asked told me the boy who had written it, his first and last name. I even knew him. How could this happen, I wondered. I told the dean of students, and after some questioning the boy confessed to the incident and was punished with a short suspension. He wasn't required to write an apology, and few adults in the community circled back to the African American students, or any students, who had been so hurt and confused by the note.

I left the school at the end of that school year. I withdrew and enrolled in a boarding school in another state. At 1,300 students, it was too big for me. I got lost in the social life, and without firm relationships with my teachers my grades began to slip. Thank goodness my parents decided to move me back to the school at the end of that 10th-grade year away. I now know that was best for me, but, Lord, back then, I was hurt, angry, and really scared. I was waiting for someone to give me the green light to say how I felt and what I needed. I wanted to say, I don't feel particularly safe here anymore, I'm not sure I feel of value, and I need to know that everything is going to be okay. When that never happened, instead of being authentic—speaking up, using my voice to ask for the support I needed, or better yet, being the change I needed to see—I pretty much put my head down and went inside myself. Instead of forgiving the hurt, I carried it on by building a bit of a wall between me and my teachers and most of my classmates.

It was during this time that I turned to literature and history, where storytelling and listening to and understanding multiple perspectives are necessary, where value is given to the voice of the most unlikely protagonist. My teachers nourished my soul in this regard, and I love them for it. I loved them for it so much that in college, I threw myself into the study of literature, history, anthropology, sociology, drama, and ultimately teaching. Out in the world I matured and gained perspective and confidence that allowed me to focus my love and knowledge on my students. And though my path was a winding one, 6 years ago it led me right back to the school. I never thought as an upper school student that I would ever be back at this school, teaching. And yet there's no place I'd rather be.

Don't let one or two negative incidents be *all* that you remember of your time in school. And likewise, don't let one or two negative incidents be all that others remember about *you*. Cliques, racist remarks, making people feel invisible, those behaviors happen everywhere. If you've received, witnessed, or even carried out any of these behaviors, stop and think how you could use your voice to help make your school a better, even stronger place. That can't happen when we build walls between us. It happens when we give others a chance to show us who they are rather than writing them off, when we welcome different people to sit next to us instead of cringe, and when we do nothing to make others feel like they are less than they are worth, because we are all a gift.

It is never too late to stand up and claim your story. You are important, and your voice matters. If you don't use your experiences to help find your voice, if you don't use your voice to state your needs or ignite a fire in this world with your wisdom, insight, or perspective because you were waiting for an invitation from someone to do so, then you are wasting a tremendous gift. This is something that has taken most of my life to figure out, and I'm continuing to figure it out, but it is because of my families, my blood family and my school family, that I have gained this wisdom.

CHAPTER 4

Language Variation in Literature

THE SECONDARY ENGLISH CLASSROOM is the synergy of two distinct traditions related to literacy and literature. Secondary English educators teach about the structure of language and about linguistic norms and conventions, and they teach students how to write for specific audiences and specific purposes. They also teach students about literature, which often tells the stories of regular people, living their lives and speaking in their varied tongues. Both of these targets emphasize the significance of communication and voice. A focus on structure and grammar allows students to examine the architecture of English and the linguistic frameworks that guide speakers and writers as they produce their prose. By examining literature, students gain appreciation for the rich diversity of language, and they are exposed to a medium through which authors and readers can grapple with critical social issues (Appleman, 2009). There is no venue more capable of addressing and embracing the concepts and issues raised in this book than the English classroom.

In this chapter, we examine how authors use language in literature that is commonly taught in secondary school classrooms. Literary texts, which are written in different modes and genres, for various audiences, and during different time periods, provide evidence of the truths of linguistic diversity. Through literature, authors tackle difficult topics, such as culture clashes, insecurity, status, and representation, in ways that are refracted through the prism of language (Bernstein, 1994). Literature is also a conduit for and a vehicle of diverse forms of expression, and language variation lends some of the richest detail and emotion. Yet, in the secondary English classroom, these texts may be challenging for some students to understand and for some educators to teach, particularly if the educators and students are less familiar with the language variations and the linguistic expressions being used. Educators who have worked with us have posed questions such as: How can we help students make sense of Shakespearean English in our contemporary era of 140-character tweets, personalized status updates, and abbreviated text messages? How can we help students who stumble when reading the dialogue in *Their Eyes Were Watching God* because they are encountering an unfamiliar language variety represented by unfamiliar spelling conventions? How can we harness the insights of other students who may be perfectly comfortable when they encounter a particular language variety in literature, without asking them to speak as a token member of or spokesperson for their assumed cultural group? The overarching question that frames this chapter thus becomes: How can educators help diverse students engage with language variation that often surfaces in texts taught in secondary English curricula? We address this question head-on and guide educators to make language variation a constructive point of conversation in the secondary English classroom.

THE IMPORTANCE OF ORALITY

The history of literature starts with the history of storytelling. In the beginning, stories were shared orally, and that spoken element still forms the backbone of literature. Characters in novels, parts in plays, and the rhythm of poetry are intertwined with the speech of a certain place and time and with the language variation of the author, narrators, and characters. From the folk tale told around a dim fire to a serial novel published in Victorian England, words in literature represent voice. Literature is uniquely suited to reflect how we talk, how language evolves, how confusions arise, how new things are said, and how words communicate through both form and meaning.

The fact that literature has its origins in oral storytelling—that is, the fact that stories come from someone's voice—distinguishes literature from the records of history. There is no attempt at objectivity alone; instead, the subject and how the subject *talks* form the story. As a result, literature allows us to know more about ourselves than about facts, figures, dates, and the movements of armies and peoples alone. *Henry V* is not just the recounting of a major battle during the Hundred Years War between England and France but also the story of soldiers and kings. *For Whom the Bell Tolls* is based on Hemingway's experience as a reporter during the Spanish Civil War but is not a memoir; he tells his story through the voices of fictional and fictionalized figures. *All Quiet on the Western Front* gives readers a picture of the trauma of the World War I battlefield from a specific young man's point of view. Through narrative, voices bring history to life and make literature captivating. As Nikki Giovanni (2002) put it, "I always loved English because whatever human beings are, we are storytellers. It is our stories that give a light to the future. . . . [H]istory is such a wonderful story of who we think we are. English is much more a story of who we really are" (p. 108).

Because literature reflects the voices of people from many different time periods, regions, and cultures, secondary English educators are likely to have heard students ask, "Why should we read this book? What's the

BOX 4.1. CURRICULAR CONNECTIONS: *The Canterbury Tales*

Chaucer's *Canterbury Tales* can provide an opportunity for students to make text-to-self connections through a focus on language. In this exercise, students can write their own tales by first selecting a location where a mix of people might come together. The students then choose people in their own lives and adapt them into characters. The characters should each have stories to tell, using authentic languages or language varieties. Perhaps students will create the grandmother's tale, the preacher's tale, the teacher's tale, the shopkeeper's tale, the friend's tale, or even the bully's tale. Once the tales are compiled, students can compare and contrast them with Chaucer's. This exercise helps students explore the ways that authors use language and language variation to indicate how diverse people communicate with one another.

point of reading literature when people don't talk like that anymore?" In part, we read to understand people other than ourselves. And, at some point not too far in the future, people won't talk like we do either. Our linguistic moment is a small part of the broad arc of communication. To read an author who talks and writes differently than we do helps us understand the flexibility that makes language, and English in particular, so fluid, innovative, and compelling.

As language continues to change—and students in the classroom are agents of that change—we see our place in a greater conversation. Chaucer wrote in Middle English and gave it legitimacy as a literary language at a time when most authors in England privileged French and Latin. Chaucer was a major influence on Shakespeare, who is often called the greatest writer in the English language. In turn, Shakespeare influenced modernist writers such as Virginia Woolf and James Joyce—who, like Shakespeare, are known for linguistic innovation and experimental style. From these and other authors, students learn that language and literature have the power to capture the human experience as part of our great tradition as thinkers, storytellers, readers, and writers. Literature, like language, is a product of who we are, where we live, the culture that surrounds us, and the time period we live in, stretching back to when the first linguistic hybrids formed the beginnings of the English language.

As stories are told from a subjective point of view, there is no standardized English formula that all literature relies upon. Instead, literature emerges from people speaking in their own manner and with their own particular usages. As many writers know, sometimes messages are better conveyed and stories are more effectively told when they are communicated with language variation. As Hamilton (1995) suggested, "[H]istorically, we have

BOX 4.2. AN EDUCATOR'S VIGNETTE: Language Variation and Oral Storytelling

Brian Higginson,
Upper School English Teacher

I teach a Folk Literature junior/senior elective in an independent high school. The course covers a range of traditional folk literature, including classic fairy tales, myths, legends, urban legends, and folk tales. We study the cultural background and the sociological and psychological implications of the tales, as well as their place in contemporary society. This year, I included a unit on the way in which the storyteller's use of language affects the delivery and reception of the tale.

Many of the tales we typically share in the English classroom come from printed versions and are, by default, told in standardized English. I began my unit on the use of language in storytelling by pointing out this fact and how it can become an unspoken norm. The students and I shared our existing understanding of what constitutes standardized English. I gave the class notes about what constitutes standardized English and what constitutes language varieties, so that we could dispel some of our unspoken assumptions and locate standardized English as one of many varieties and one with specific purposes.

We then went on to talk in general terms about our emotional or instinctive reactions to nonstandardized language varieties. My students were aware of and were able to articulate many of the stereotypes and prejudices about many of them. I then encouraged students to look at how nonstandardized varieties can also be useful and appropriate mediums for the telling of different kinds of tales. All stories would have been told originally in one variation or another. As stories have traveled around the world, they have morphed considerably, and this process depends largely on the language—or, in the English-speaking world, the language variation—of the teller. I gave students a printed version of a story told in the localized variety of the Scots traveler folk (collected by Duncan Williamson) together with a glossary of terms, and I asked my students to mark as many examples of nonstandardized English as they could find. I also frequently told my own tales in my nonstandard dialect of British English, and we listened to tales told in American English varieties, particularly Southern English, Appalachian English, and African American English.

My students, who are almost exclusively White and middle-class, got to listen to a range of voices in these different tales. In our debriefing sessions, one of the conclusions we reached is that to hear or see a traditional story in dialect adds authenticity to a tale. My students also commented on the way that language variation can add humor and authority. They noted the warmth and welcoming tone of these tales, as opposed to the relative distancing effect of more formal, standardized English.

We also applied these ideas to "real-life" contexts in which a choice can be made between standardized English and a variation. I challenged each student to tell a self-selected tale with particular attention to the conscious use of either standardized English or nonstandardized English. (For most of my students, this was the use of informal slang.) We finished with a session on the privileges afforded to speakers of standardized English. This was a surprise to the students, and, I think, an eye-opener for them. Overall, this unit was a useful and informative lens through which to look at oral tradition and to examine storytelling as an interesting context in which to study language variation.

placed such a low value on some regional or cultural dialects that we have often blinded ourselves to the human insight articulated through them; conversely, we place such a strong value on so-called standard English dialect that we often assume wisdom in banality" (p. 110). Simply because standardized English is often the prestige language variety (see Chapter 2) does not mean that it is always the most persuasive variety or the variety best suited to convey meaning, voice, personality, range of emotion, and the depth of human experience. Secondary English educators are well positioned to explore with students the question of when it is useful to communicate in standardized English compared to other varieties of English. When students explore how different varieties of English have been used in various genres of literature and to what effect, students build their own understanding of voice and tone and consider how they employ different styles of communication, in speech and writing.

AUTHORIAL CHOICE AND LITERARY VOICE

In great literature, an author's choice of words is never an accident. Each word is carefully chosen, in content and form. Tone, euphemisms, figures of speech, word choice, and other elements are therefore ideal subjects for academic exploration. It is no accident that Hamlet's speech differs from the Gravediggers, who tell jokes and parody legal jargon, or that Shakespeare's strong female characters Portia, Beatrice, and Desdemona deliver powerful, persuasive speeches. In *Adventures of Huckleberry Finn*, Mark Twain represents social class and racial politics in Southern society by having Huck Finn's speech differ from Tom Sawyer's and by having Huck's and Tom's speech differ markedly from Jim's.

An author's choice to use language variation is important, not just within the context of literature, but also for readers and speakers in the real world. The question of how people talk, in literature and in life, is a central question for the secondary English classroom. Some authors who incorporate language variation into their literary works seek to highlight the speech and culture of those who are different from themselves. Others use language variation to convey something about their personal speech habits. Whether authors represent the linguistic traditions of another culture or their own, the question of who speaks for whom is always pertinent.

Who Speaks for Whom?

In the preface to *Adventures of Huckleberry Finn*, Mark Twain provides the following note:

> In this book a number of dialects are used, to wit: the Missouri negro dialect; the extremest form of the backwoods Southwestern dialect; the ordinary "Pike County" dialect; and four modified varieties of this last. The shadings have not been done in a haphazard fashion, or by guesswork; but painstakingly, and with the trustworthy guidance and support of personal familiarity with these several forms of speech.
>
> I make this explanation for the reason that without it many readers would suppose that all these characters were trying to talk alike and not succeeding.
>
> THE AUTHOR.

As Twain explained, he intentionally incorporated language variation into his novel in order to portray specific linguistic and cultural elements. How authors style the speech of characters who are different from themselves can provide food for thought about how "the Other" is depicted in literature. For instance, in *Adventures of Huckleberry Finn*, Jim, a former slave who has been freed, is unquestionably portrayed as "the Other." As readers, we learn of his status from the way Jim is described in the text and, most dramatically, from his dialogue, which is interspersed with spellings that are intended to represent the pronunciations of an uneducated man who speaks in a Southern variety of African American English. Yet, Jim also speaks with moral clarity and criticizes the injustice of Southern society at that time. Indeed, Mark Twain found it more politically feasible to use the voice of Jim to challenge the prevailing social mores, rather than placing those words in the mouths of characters whose language is closer to the norms of standardized English.

Nonstandardized varieties are often used in creative works to lend character and personality, to reveal attitudes, or to represent some social or cultural fact about the speaker in question. For instance, in *The Hobbit*, Tolkien used Cockney speech to portray the trolls as "dissipated, snarling, pirate types, with a jug of grog between them" (Anderson & Groff, 1972, pp. 25–26). Many authors have a character speak in a variety that comes across as uneducated or inarticulate in order to demonstrate that character's ignorance or lack of intelligence. To use nonstandardized varieties of

BOX 4.3. AN EDUCATOR'S VIGNETTE: Teaching About *To Kill a Mockingbird*

Jessica Shildt,
9th-Grade English Teacher

I created a lesson for my 9th-grade students to analyze language variation in *To Kill a Mockingbird* as part of their critical reading of the novel. I introduced students to the concepts of dialect, linguistic bias, and style shifting, drawing from the *Voices of North Carolina* dialect awareness curriculum (Reaser & Wolfram, 2007). The students were very responsive to these concepts and connected them to their own lives. Several students identified and commented upon how members of their family spoke, and several cited examples of style shifting.

I then asked students to apply these concepts to our reading of the novel. Students discussed dialogue and dialect, including what they felt the dialogue added to the novel, what effect recreating dialect had on the novel, and what difficulties Harper Lee might have faced when trying to recreate dialect in the novel. They also explored what linguistic differences they noticed in the characters' dialogue and how we might explain those differences.

We talked about register, which is a part of the overall diction of the novel. In one passage, Calpurnia explains that she uses one language variety at church and a different one when she is with the Finches: "Now what if I talked white-folks' talk at church, and with my neighbors? They'd think I was puttin' on airs to beat Moses." Students also explored the provocative passage in which Scout comments that Calpurnia has "command over two languages" and in which Jem and Scout ask Calpurnia why she speaks in different dialects "when you know it's not right." I asked students whether they agreed with Jem and Scout's reasoning or with Calpurnia's, and we discussed whether one dialect of English is "better" than any other.

We also used *To Kill a Mockingbird* to talk about linguistic bias. Across my classes, students were quick to associate certain ways of speaking with lack of education and lack of intelligence. At the same time, students noted that although Calpurnia speaks in a less standard dialect, she is nevertheless intelligent. The difference between education and intelligence was a difficult nuance for some students to grasp, while for others it was an obvious assertion. I suspect that some students struggled because they did not consider that people might have different levels of access to formal education.

As reflected in these comments, students in my classes arrived at well-formulated opinions about the importance of using standard English in certain situations while accepting and embracing language variation and understanding its role in society. I also liked this unit because, in addition to being such an important topic, it was a good way to prompt students to do close readings of specific quotations. I would definitely teach about language variation in *To Kill a Mockingbird* again.

English as shorthand to represent a character's nature or social circumstances can be a tricky endeavor, however, and one that is fraught with political and cultural difficulties. When an author decides how to portray a character, which languages or language varieties are chosen for that character's speech, and how does the author make that choice? Assumptions can easily make their way into literary representations, and these representations affect readers. Readers form mental pictures of literary characters based on whether they like or dislike the language that the characters use. If readers like a particular character and that character's language, they tend to ascribe positive traits to that character—and vice versa, which can lead to bias and stereotyping (Carr, 1974, p. 88).

It is important for students to think critically about the language attitudes (and, by proxy, the cultural beliefs) that are reflected in literature. Students can consider questions such as: What accents are used to portray different types of characters? Are these representations fair or not? What might happen if readers make incorrect assumptions about speakers based on their language? The close study of the linguistic choices that authors make can build students' skills of literary analysis and their critical language awareness. A multicultural education perspective supports teaching students to value linguistic diversity, just as students should be taught to value differences and diversity along the lines of gender, race/ethnicity, social class, and the like. As the National Council of Teachers of English and the International Reading Association (1996) stated, "Schools are responsible for creating a climate of respect for the variety of languages that students speak and the variety of cultures from which they come" (p. 42). In other words, there is a clear impetus to discuss with students how linguistic representations can influence readers' attitudes and expectations about characters and cultures.

The Use of Eye Dialect

Authors who want to convey language variation in literature face the question of how to do so. One common method is the use of *eye dialect*, the written technique of spelling words to suggest how they sound when they are pronounced (Carr, 1974)—for example, *wimmin* for *women*, *sed* for *said*, and *enuff* for *enough*. This practice is called eye dialect because spelling is used to convey a specific pronunciation, so that the dialect strikes the *eye* (through the printed word) rather than appealing to the ear (through sound or more accurate phonetic representation).

American fiction is well known for the use of eye dialect, as seen in the Uncle Remus tales, the plays of Eugene O'Neill and Tennessee Williams, and novels such as *Adventures of Huckleberry Finn*, *The Color Purple*, *The*

> **BOX 4.4. CURRICULAR CONNECTIONS:**
> **Eye Dialect in *Their Eyes Were Watching God***
>
> The following passage in *Their Eyes Were Watching God* by Zora Neale Hurston illustrates the technique of eye dialect, as seen in such spellings as *wid* for *with*, *dey* for *they*, and *yo'* for *your*.
>
> "Now, Pheoby, don't feel too mean wid de rest of 'em 'cause dey's parched up from not knowin' things. Dem meatskins is got tuh rattle tuh make out they's alive. Let 'em consolate theyselves wid talk. 'Course, talkin' don't amount tuh uh hill uh beans when yuh can't do nothin' else. And listenin' tuh dat kind uh talk is jus' lak openin' yo' mouth and lettin' de moon shine down yo' throat."
>
> Students and educators can examine this and other passages and analyze Hurston's use of eye dialect. How are alternative spellings used by Hurston to represent language variation? In what ways does the use of eye dialect lend linguistic flavor to the text? What challenges might accompany the use of eye dialect, in Hurston's works or in those of other authors?

Grapes of Wrath, and *Their Eyes Were Watching God*. Contemporary novels that have been spotlighted for the use of eye dialect include *A Confederacy of Dunces* and *The Help*. There is also a strong tradition of using eye dialect in British literature: for example, in the novels of Dickens, such as *Bleak House* and *David Copperfield*; in George Bernard Shaw's *Pygmalion*, where the diction of Liza is the central theme of the play; and in the *Harry Potter* series, in which J. K. Rowling uses eye dialect for the speech of several characters, notably Hagrid. In many of the greatest literary works, which are often read in secondary English classrooms, authors use eye dialect to portray the voices of their characters.

One benefit of the use of eye dialect is that it immediately announces to the reader the fact that a particular character speaks differently than others in a given text. Authors may use eye dialect with the goal of lending authenticity to their work or to introduce readers to a language variety that they may not otherwise have been familiar with (Peterson, 1984). Without the use of eye dialect, readers might lose a sense of the nature of the speech that authors are trying to represent; for example, many students report that they would never have known how Huck and Jim were supposed to sound if Mark Twain had not used eye dialect.

One objection to the use of eye dialect is on the linguistic grounds that it is impossible to perfectly reproduce spoken language in writing (Minnick, 2004). Often, eye dialect is inconsistently or ambiguously written, and despite authors' best efforts, it may not accurately or reliably represent the language variety in question. What is spelled *wuz* in one passage may be spelled *was* in another, even in the same piece of literature. Educators can encourage students to consider what is gained and what is lost when a character is portrayed using eye dialect. Why use nonstandardized spellings such as *sed* for *said* and *enuff* for *enough* when this is how most speakers would pronounce these words? Are there ways to portray a particular character without using eye dialect, or is this tool necessary? If so, how much eye dialect should be used? Should the author try to represent every nonstandardized pronunciation, or only some, and on what basis are those decisions made?

Sometimes, when authors represent the speech of people from a different culture, especially in cases when the author has had only limited experience with this group, the use of eye dialect can reflect assumptions and prejudices, rather than representing actual features of authentic speech. In these circumstances, readers may feel that this use of eye dialect is stereotypical or even that it is reminiscent of language used in a minstrel show. For instance, the fact that some authors portray the language of African American characters by using eye dialect but represent the speech of White characters with standardized English has been the subject of much critical analysis. Consider the novels *To Kill a Mockingbird*, *Uncle Tom's Cabin*, and *The Help*, which were written by White authors. Some readers have no problem with the authors' use of eye dialect, but others feel that it plays into linguistic stereotyping and caricature of African Americans. In contrast, in *Beloved*, Toni Morrison uses eye dialect to represent the speech of some of the White characters but uses standardized English to represent the thoughts and speech of the book's main character, who is African American.

Questions of authenticity and representation might prompt students to consider who is a native speaker of a given language variety or a native authority on a given culture. Should authors represent a language variety that they did not grow up speaking or a culture they were not a part of? Do students feel that the words and worlds these authors portray are realistic? Tensions surrounding who has the power to name, label, and represent can arise in literature, where authors control voice, tone, and point of view. How these elements are received and analyzed is open to debate and will vary from reader to reader. It is important to provide a forum—whether in class, online, or in journals—where students can express and analyze their responses to literature.

An additional critique is that eye dialect is often used to indicate that a given character is uneducated (Rickford & Rickford, 2000, p. 23). This conflation of language variation and lack of education is an incorrect assumption. Automatically equating language variation with lower education and intelligence contradicts our third linguistic truth, because language differences are not indicators of deficit but rather are natural and normal variations. Without being guided to have conversations about the pros and cons of how and why an author is representing language variation in a given way, secondary English students who encounter eye dialect may not have the tools to critically examine it or understand the social and cultural politics involved in an author's choice to use it. Unless discussion establishes the opposite, students may erroneously come to believe that there is a one-to-one correlation between the way someone talks and thinks, and they may assume that a character who uses nonstandardized English is necessarily less educated or less smart than one who uses standardized English. As Carr (1974) succinctly explained,

> Consider the fact that in most American classrooms children are conditioned to believe that misspelling is bad and often gain the connotation that if one cannot spell correctly one is unintelligent. It could be that as children read literature containing "eye dialect" they notice the "misspelled" words and, applying the conditioning of the spelling class, use them as indicators of the intelligence or "lack of quality" of the characters shown as *speaking* the misspelled words. In other words, the child is not, perhaps, aware of the device as a literary tool but actually attributes the "misspelling" to the character and considers him a "country yokel," unintelligent or even undesirable. (pp. 81–82)

For these reasons, readers often object entirely to the use of eye dialect, because they believe (perhaps correctly, perhaps incorrectly) that the author is using nonstandardized spellings to indicate the ignorance of a given character and culture. It is easy to see that students might draw the same conclusions.

There is danger in immediately condemning the use of eye dialect as a tool of insensitivity or oppression, however. "[W]e must not consider a book as racist simply because it is written in dialect for to do so would be to ignore the fact that many distinct and communicative varieties of our language do exist and that no one prestige dialect is to be found within the United States," Carr (1974) asserted. "[O]ral dialects are often misrepresented in literature," and being aware of such misrepresentations can help students acquire the critical awareness "necessary to notice inaccuracies and stereotypes which might be demeaning or unfair to groups represented within the literature" (p. 87). In sum, there are many different stances on the pros and cons of eye dialect, and there is no right or wrong answer to the question of its use in literature. Because students will certainly be exposed to it, it is important to discuss where, why, how, and to what effect authors incorporate language variation into their works.

Eye dialect is not the only technique that authors can use to indicate that a character or narrator speaks in a particular language variety. Dufresne (2003), who suggested that authors avoid the use of eye dialect, recommended that authors achieve linguistic effect "by the rhythm of the prose, by the syntax, the diction, idioms and figures of speech, by the vocabulary indigenous to the locale" (p. 200). Such techniques can signal language diversity without using nonstandardized spellings.

Flannery O'Connor is an excellent example of how to use these techniques. O'Connor sometimes used eye dialect to represent Southern pronunciations, as in "Hep that lady up, Hiram" in "A Good Man Is Hard to Find," "Wheerd you git that turkey?" in "The Turkey," and "I want to innerduce you to the True Prophet here" in *Wise Blood*. But for the most part O'Connor felt that writers should use eye dialect sparingly, and as a result she tended to use Southernisms that do not rely on this technique. For instance, she frequently used nonstandardized grammatical features, as in "I don't reckon you know anything about it, you ain't even married" in "A Stroke of Good Fortune" and "I'll tell you another thing, Hulga, you ain't so smart. I been believing in nothing ever since I was born!" in "Good Country People." Southern-inflected idioms, metaphors, turns of phrase, vocabulary, names, nicknames, and place names are also a fixture of her literary works, and these Southernisms appear in O'Connor's own letters (Fitzgerald, 1979, p. xiv). In fact, O'Connor is quoted as saying, "If my characters speak Southern, it's because I do" (Magee, 2000, p. 112).

Much great American literature is written with a Southern style and voice, and Southern writers—"the epicenter of the American narrative voice" (Ferris, 2011)—are often masters of adding regional flavor to their texts through the use of language. In *Light in August*, for example, Faulkner uses vocabulary items such as *reckon*, *muck*, *right smart*, and *aim* (to mean *intend*), along with nonstandardized grammatical features, to lend Southern flair (e.g., "What are you fixing to do with your eggmoney," "I wouldn't care for none," and "Like he hadn't never been to bed, even"). Like O'Connor, Faulkner occasionally used eye dialect to represent nonstandardized pronunciations, such as *sho* for *sure* and *Miz* for *Miss*, but he often did not overtly indicate that he was writing with a particular pronunciation in mind. In *Light in August*, it may not be immediately apparent to readers who are unfamiliar with the Mississippi variety of Southern English of that time period that the names *Birch* and *Bunch* would be pronounced in similar ways, yet this resemblance is the very basis for the character Lena making her journey to the town of Jefferson.

In *To Kill a Mockingbird*, Harper Lee did use eye dialect, as in *chillun* for *children* and *nome* for *no ma'am*, but she also used nonstandardized verb forms (*you bringing* for *you are bringing*) and phrases (*my stars*, *sit a spell*) to indicate that her characters used Southern English. Jessica Shildt, the 9th-grade English educator profiled in Box 4.3 on p. 79, also explored Harper Lee's use of Southern idioms with her students. Students found and analyzed idioms, such as "three bricks shy of a load," "faster than greased lightning," and "madder than a wet hen," as examples of figurative language characteristic of Southern English. Many linguistic choices—not only eye dialect—are available to authors who want to incorporate language variation into their texts, and secondary English educators can discuss with students the range of techniques they can expect to find, particularly in Southern literature.

In the secondary English classroom, research has found many benefits to examining language variation in literature. The use of multicultural literature has been shown to increase students' awareness for other cultures and to enhance their competency in language arts and even their reading comprehension (Craig & Washington, 2006; Meier, 2008), and, in much the same way, when students encounter language varieties, it helps them "[develop] awareness of and empathy with multicultural voices" (Traugott, 1999, p. 176). Understanding language variation can foster among students "a greater understanding of, and appreciation for, the various forms of American English"; it can "discourage the formation of stereotypes and misconceptions towards persons based on language and . . . encourage tolerance and perspective, if not pride, toward the interesting variants of our language" (Carr, 1974, p. 88). As the National Council of Teachers of English (2003) recommended, educators should select culturally diverse materials that will "expose students to new horizons and should increase their awareness and heighten their perceptions of the social reality. Classroom reading materials can be employed to further our students' reading ability and, at the same time, can familiarize them with other varieties of English" (p. 10).

Given the complexities involved in linguistic representation in literature, it is important for educators and students to examine how authors represent speakers and cultures through linguistic and literary techniques (Christianson, 2002). In Box 4.5 on p. 86, we provide discussion questions that focus students' attention on representation rather than authenticity. As Minnick (2004) explained, because the written word can never represent the spoken word with complete accuracy, "the best practitioners of literary dialect create effects that are linguistically and artistically believable" (p. 33). The central question for educators and students is therefore not whether an author has represented speech with perfect accuracy, as no such objective measure is possible. Rather, the focus should be on "what can be learned about how writers and readers interpret and understand language variation" (p. 54). With this perspective, students interrogate the authorial choice behind the voice—the author's purpose and intent, the literary effect of the use of language, the linguistic context that surrounds the literature, and the politics that are involved in any linguistic and cultural representation.

As students analyze authorial choice in language representation, they build their awareness of language diversity, and they build competency in

BOX 4.5. CURRICULAR CONNECTIONS: Analyzing the Role of Eye Dialect in Literature

In the secondary English classroom, educators and students can analyze the role of eye dialect by focusing on how an author uses language to explore the relationship between identity, representation, and culture in a literary work. Some discussion questions that educators might prompt students to consider are:

- How is language used, in positive and negative ways, to portray people from different cultures?
- Who are the intended and the unintended audiences for the literary work, and how might these audiences affect the language that is used?
- What is the author's relationship to the language variety being portrayed, and does the author make claims about authenticity or representation? If so, how would you evaluate those claims?
- What appears to be the intention behind the author's use of language variation? How does the use of language variation reflect, reinforce, or challenge social and linguistic attitudes?
- Is eye dialect used, and if so, how might it affect readers' views of different characters? What is its effectiveness or persuasive appeal, particularly if the author uses eye dialect to represent some trait or aspect of a character?
- Would the literary work have the same effect if eye dialect were not used?
- Is it acceptable for an author to be a language inventor, writing what strikes the imagination without necessarily grounding the representation in reality? Is it acceptable for an author to be a language voyeur, portraying the speech of others who are "exotic" in some way, or should authors be journalists or historians who strictly document what they hear?

English language arts. As they learn about nonstandardized varieties of English, how authors use them, and to what effect, students can better analyze literary elements such as word choice, style, and tone, which, in turn, can help students make purposeful and effective choices and rich interpretations in their own communication. These benefits are also established, for example, in the standards for Advanced Placement English Language and Composition courses (College Board, 2010). Literature can therefore be used in the secondary English classroom to help students understand how writers make rhetorical and linguistic choices with resulting stylistic effects; this insight, then, supports the development of all students' English language skills.

BOX 4.6. A SOCIOLINGUIST'S VIGNETTE: The Linguistic and Cultural Realities of Language Variation in Literature

Dr. Lisa Cohen Minnick,
Associate Professor of English at Western Michigan University

Many of the English education majors in my classes say they are attracted to the profession because they enjoy literature and excel in their English courses. But before taking my class, "Language Variation in American English," most of them take for granted a key factor in their success: their proficiency in standard English. Nearly all are native speakers of standard English, but most have never thought about what this has meant for them as students and what it will mean for their own students when they become teachers themselves.

Academic success depends on proficiency in standard English, of course, and so students from standard-speaking homes start off with a clear advantage. One of our first conversations in my Language Variation course is about how this advantage works. "Imagine that you are a student whose language of nurture is not standard English," I suggest. "You are expected to read a language variety that sounds different from what you are used to hearing and seems to function differently in some ways too. Maybe your teacher interrupts and corrects you—in front of everyone—when you speak or read aloud in class. Maybe your work comes back covered in corrections. How do you feel about school? How do you feel about yourself?"

Smart, compassionate people that these English education majors are, they want to know right away how they can help students achieve proficiency in standard English without causing them hurt or disrespecting their linguistic and cultural traditions. My suggestion is to start with their own speech and particularly with their attitudes about it. Like most speakers, my students have come to believe that standard English is "correct" English and that everything else is therefore wrong, ungrammatical, deviant, or (at best) of limited acceptability. And why wouldn't they believe that? They've been hearing it all their lives.

In this context, literature that visually represents "dialectal" speech can be a valuable teaching tool, but it can also be problematic. "I don't know how to read this!" students struggling with written representations of dialect will say. "I can't understand it!" And thus *intelligibility* becomes the frame within which literary dialect is explored. "Try reading it out loud," teachers often suggest. "It will sound more familiar to you than it looks, and you will get better at reading it."

They are right about that. But there is also more to it. Engagement with literary dialect requires engagement with linguistics. When the focus is primarily (or entirely) on decoding what is being said by characters whose speech is represented in dialect, it becomes an exercise in *translation*, a framing that emphasizes *difference*. Deciphering the literal meaning of what is being said becomes an end in itself, and the students often move on without considering what the dialectal representations are actually *doing* in the text.

For example, what should readers make of a text in which the speech of some characters is visually marked as "dialectal" while the speech of other characters is represented as "standard"? What might the visual marking of speech suggest about the roles and status of characters whose speech is marked, including in relation to characters whose speech is unmarked and to the intended audience?

Consider, for example, Mark Twain's *The Adventures of Tom Sawyer* and its sequel, *Adventures of Huckleberry Finn*. In *Tom Sawyer*, the character of Huck Finn functions in part as a foil to Tom, a middle-class White child who is a mischief-maker but who regularly attends school and church and lives under the watchful eye of his loving but strict Aunt Polly. Huck, on the other hand, is the homeless, motherless child of the no-account town drunk, who is mostly absent from his son's life and violently abusive when he is present. The local moms order their own children to avoid Huck, and the way his speech is represented in both novels helps to serve as a visual reminder of his outsider status.

It is important to note that these types of marked features occur in Huck's speech at significantly lower frequencies in the novel that bears his own name than in *Tom Sawyer*. There could be any number of explanations for this difference, of course, but it is interesting to consider in light of the prominence in *Huckleberry Finn* of a major character who is African American and whose speech is represented as highly dialectal. The character of Jim, an escaped slave, uses much higher frequencies of vernacular features than does Huck, even for features that the two speakers would almost certainly have shared, such as pronunciation of words ending in *-ing* as *-in*, as suggested by spellings such as *goin'* for *going*. The *-in* pronunciations were common among Black as well as White speakers of all social classes in 19th-century Missouri, the setting for both novels (Pederson, 1965). And of course students will recognize that *-in* pronunciations continue to flourish across social, racial, ethnic, and regional demographics in present-day American English as well.

A number of critics have charged that the characterization of Jim is based on racist stereotypes popularized in minstrel shows that were common in Twain's time and into the 20th century (see Lott, 1995; Morrison, 1998). Some of these critics point specifically to Jim's vernacular speech as a constant visual reminder of his status as "Other," even compared to Huck, who is also an outsider in his own right. Possible explanations for why Huck's speech is represented in the later novel as so much less "dialectal" than Jim's (and less so than Huck's own speech in *Tom Sawyer*) are complex, but as I have discussed elsewhere (Minnick, 2004, 2010), *Huckleberry Finn* positions Huck, linguistically and otherwise, as the narrative center and defines other characters in relation to him. This is not surprising in a book that bears his name. But it is problematic in that it presents Jim—but not Huck, who is White—as existing in a space outside what is presented as the normal community of speakers, even though it is clear from both novels that Huck's lived experience also takes place very much outside that community.

Conversations with these themes are worth having with students. Learning about language variation in general and about African American English in particular, including how it works as well as where it came from, can open a challenging, provocative, and problematic text like *Huckleberry Finn* to new readings that have important and valuable things to say to students from all linguistic backgrounds. Students whose language of nurture is something other than standard English sometimes initially find literary dialect troubling or alienating but later often discover that a linguistically informed approach is engaging and empowering. It can also inspire standard-speaking students to explore their own linguistic privilege, which they are otherwise rarely if ever asked to explore. By considering the distance, linguistic and otherwise, between standard-speaking characters and those whose speech is marked in ways that echo as well as reinforce real-life social and linguistic chasms, students can identify and inquire into powerful cultural values and assumptions, such as that Whiteness, middle-class status, and standard speech are universally desirable.

Literary dialect bears witness to the evolution of beliefs and attitudes about language varieties and their speakers. As an educational tool, analysis of literary dialect presents opportunities for students to examine mechanisms through which standardized English is authorized and its speakers empowered, often at the expense of linguistic minorities. Considered in these contexts, literary dialect is uniquely situated to help students understand how language ideologies drive social valuations that attach to different classes of speakers in texts and in real life. Literary dialect can also help them to understand how some authors use dialect as a means to subvert these ideologies. Teaching literary dialect can thus help students inquire critically into language ideologies as well as understand literary works in new ways. However, teachers must bring to the task a comprehensive understanding of the linguistic and cultural realities of variation.

Writing Our Own Identities

We have discussed the issues involved when authors use language variation to describe characters who are "other" than them, linguistically and culturally. Language variation can also be used to tell readers something about the author's own identity and how they assert their linguistic agency. Particularly for members of linguistically marginalized groups, the use of nonstandardized varieties of English can be a powerful marker of in-group identity, and authors can use different varieties of English to communicate something about the cultures and places they come from.

Charles Dickens provides an excellent illustration of the theme of language and identity, because of his ability to capture the language of characters from divergent walks of life that was often based on his own experiences. Some of Dickens' most memorable characters are those who inhabit debtors' prisons and poorhouses. When Dickens was young, his father, mother, and younger siblings were imprisoned at Marshalsea debtors' prison for several months, and Dickens often spent days there with them. This prison provided the backdrop for *Little Dorrit*, and the language of the prison world informs nearly every one of Dickens' novels. In fact, Dickens helped bring into mainstream usage many words that had been associated with the working class or the criminal underworld and that were considered earthy or vulgar (Zimmer, 2012). Dickens also drew upon his personal experiences doing menial labor at a boot-blacking factory to lend authenticity to his descriptions of the industrial life of Victorian England. Due to his father's missteps, Dickens was well aware of how the courts operated. He wrote about legal wrangling and its victims in novels such as *Bleak House*, and *David Copperfield* is a thinly veiled autobiographical novel of Dickens' early years. In Dickens' novels, readers hear the sounds, words, and phrases of impoverished Victorian England as well as the language of the upper classes. The distinctive voices of the characters reflect the sounds that Dickens heard, from his childhood through rising to become the most prominent writer of his generation. Dickens is an exemplar for how to write about themes that are personally meaningful and how to use language that reflects the social worlds that an author aims to portray.

Language choice is integral to writing autobiographical or semi-autobiographical narratives, and students can be guided to think about how best to express their own histories and life experiences. By thinking about the role of language choice in writing about identity, students can consider how authors from all walks of life use language and literature to examine who we are and where we come from. Appalachian scholars, for instance, have endorsed using regional literature that incorporates elements of Appalachian English in secondary classrooms, because it can help engage students in the curriculum by connecting to their own lives (Waitt, 2006).

Another exemplar in relation to the theme of language and identity is the poet Paul Laurence Dunbar. As the only African American in his high school, Dunbar became acutely aware of language differences in his community of Dayton, Ohio. As a result, in his poetry, he sought to show the beauty of African American English as well as the standardized English that is commonly used in poetry of the European tradition. His confidence in using both varieties inspired later African American poets, including Langston Hughes, to do the same. In Dunbar's poetry, the choice of which variety to use is tied to the themes that the poem reflects. Through language variation, Dunbar challenges readers to consider how their backgrounds and social worlds compare to the circumstances he portrays. Some readers might find similarities between their own language and Dunbar's use of standardized English. Others might find that their language has more in common with Dunbar's use of African American English. Some might be perfectly comfortable with both. When encountering language variation in poetry, as in any text, readers either recognize voices that seem familiar, or they encounter voices that seem unfamiliar or strange. In the secondary English classroom, the task is to engage with the known and the unknown, recognizing the importance of listening to and learning from messages that are communicated in different ways.

Consider also the author Zora Neale Hurston, whose works are routinely included in secondary English curricula. Many of her characters talk in ways that mirror the speech of people Hurston grew up with in Alabama and Florida. Other characters represent the people Hurston studied as an ethnographer and folklorist. In her literary works, Hurston made extensive use of eye dialect, and many contemporary scholars have deemed her representation of language to be authentic and impressive. Over half of *Their Eyes Were Watching God* is quoted speech, and Hurston used eye dialect within the dialogue to help establish the value of oral tradition and storytelling (Minnick, 2004). As we saw in Box 4.4 on p. 81, eye dialect can be seen in such lines as, "Let 'em consolate theyselves wid talk. 'Course, talkin' don't amount tuh uh hill uh beans when yuh can't do nothin' else." According to Holloway (1987), "Within the [black] dialect, in its sound, its structures, and its meanings, the culture of a people is preserved and protected. Within the artistry of Hurston, this oral culture is rendered literate" (p. 114).

Though routinely praised today, Zora Neale Hurston's use of eye dialect was not always well received, particularly by other African American writers of her time (Minnick, 2004). Some of them felt that the use of nonstandard spelling played into stereotypical portrayals of African Americans, and they objected to Hurston using eye dialect because it was a tool that White writers had used to misrepresent Black speech (Minnick, 2004). Paul Laurence Dunbar similarly felt torn about reactions to his use of language variation. Although he had been praised for the way his poems represented the speech of his community, and although he is quoted as saying "my natural speech is dialect," Dunbar was wary of being pigeonholed as a "dialect poet" and worried that his use of language variation would play into stereotypes of African Americans (Nettels, 1988, pp. 72, 83).

When authors represent their own linguistic and cultural traditions, it is no less complex a situation than when authors portray those of others. The range with which African American writers approach language variation in their literature is broad, and educators can encourage students to think about the complexities of cultural representation. Some African American authors employ eye dialect to represent African American culture and to promote African American literature (for example, Zora Neale Hurston, as part of the Harlem Renaissance). In other literature written by African

BOX 4.7. CURRICULAR CONNECTIONS: The Poetry of Paul Laurence Dunbar and Langston Hughes

Paul Laurence Dunbar and Langston Hughes, both African American poets, used different language varieties—African American English as well as the type of standardized English often used in poetry of the European tradition—to portray mood, theme, voice, and emotion.

In Dunbar's poem "I Continue to Dream" (seen in the following excerpt), the use of standardized English is part of his representation of ambition and hope:

I take my dreams and make of them a bronze vase
and a round fountain with a beautiful statue in its center.
And a song with a broken heart and I ask you:
Do you understand my dreams?

In comparison, in the poem "A Negro Love Song" (seen in the following excerpt), language variation is used to represent the voices of everyday men and women, engaged in everyday interactions, such as courtship, during the time period in which Dunbar was writing.

Seen my lady home las' night,
Jump back, honey, jump back.
Hel' huh han' an' sque'z it tight,
Jump back, honey, jump back.
Hyeahd huh sigh a little sigh,
Seen a light gleam f'om huh eye,
An' a smile go flittin' by —
Jump back, honey, jump back.

Similar themes surface in the poetry of Langston Hughes. In the poem "Theme for English B," Hughes uses standardized English to tell the story of writing his biography for a homework assignment.

So will my page be colored that I write?
Being me, it will not be white.
But it will be
a part of you, instructor.
You are white—
yet a part of me, as I am a part of you.
That's American.

In comparison, in the poem "Mother to Son" (seen in the following excerpt), Hughes uses language variation to establish the mother's voice and lend emotional depth to her character.

Well, son, I'll tell you:
Life for me ain't been no crystal stair. . . .
Don't you fall now—

For I'se still goin', honey,
I'se still climbin',
And life for me ain't been no crystal stair.

On our website, www.charityhudleymallinson.com/wdl/, educators and students can listen to poems by Dunbar and Hughes and consider: How does the use of language variation and/or the use of standardized English establish tone in a poem? What specific linguistic features are used (for example, as discussed in Charity Hudley & Mallinson, 2011)? Would a poem written in African American English have a different meaning or resonance if it were written in standardized English and vice versa? How do the styles of Dunbar and Hughes compare to each other? Students can compose their own poems that, like those of Dunbar and Hughes, differ in the use of varieties of English and explain how the linguistic choices they made helped them accomplish their literary goals.

Americans—for instance, in the slave narrative *Incidents in the Life of a Slave Girl*, by Harriet Jacobs, and in the poetry of Rita Dove and Nikki Giovanni—eye dialect is sometimes used and sometimes not. In her short story "The Lesson," Toni Cade Bambara adds cultural nuance to how the African American characters speak through the use of vocabulary and idiomatic expressions, and she rarely uses nonstandardized spellings (Heller, 2003). In *A Lesson Before Dying*, by Ernest Gaines, both standardized English and African American English are used in dialogue to help differentiate the characters and reveal their social status (Rickford & Young, 2010). For authors, the process of writing their identities into their literature is imbued with the same identity questions that we face in our everyday lives. Literature explores the human experience, not only relationships and connections but also divisions and tensions.

Controversial Language, Complex Topics

As seen in lists of banned books and discussions about what to include in curricula, literature is often steeped in praise and in controversy. One of the most challenging topics is when characters speak in ways that readers find objectionable. Secondary English educators are routinely faced with explaining to students why an author chooses to have characters discuss distasteful topics or use hateful words. How can educators talk about controversial language and weighty social issues in ways that are linguistically and culturally informed?

Educators often feel uncomfortable discussing the n-word, which surfaces in many literary works on secondary English reading lists, including *Adventures of Huckleberry Finn*, *Beloved*, *Invisible Man*, *Of Mice and Men*,

Their Eyes Were Watching God, *To Kill a Mockingbird*, and *Uncle Tom's Cabin*. As one 9th-grade English educator who has worked with us said, when she teaches *To Kill a Mockingbird*, "there's always the issue of racial slurs." Other educators have similarly questioned what message is sent in *Adventures of Huckleberry Finn* and in the stories of Flannery O'Connor, where White authors use the n-word to reflect issues about race and racism in the South, wondering whether it is enough to tell students "that's how people spoke back then" and whether terms like the n-word should be censored from literature that is taught in the secondary English classroom.

Controversial language in literature—including the n-word, other ethnic and religious slurs, gendered terms such as *bitch*, and curse words—can provide a rich opportunity to engage students with texts and make connections between literature and their own lives. Rather than shying away from it and the challenging and sensitive themes it can raise, conversations about controversial language can allow classroom discussions to run deeper. Baker (2011), a middle school language arts teacher in Missouri, described her experience when a discussion about the n-word in *Of Mice and Men* led her class to debate censorship. When she asked her 8th-graders, "If I could have given you a copy of *Of Mice and Men* that did not have the n-word, should I have done so?" she received a range of answers. Most of her students said no, arguing that they were mature enough to deal with the term, that they have already encountered it in their everyday lives, that they look to their teachers to teach about such language, and that censorship erases part of history. One student, a 14-year-old African American girl named Jordan, disagreed. She explained that she wanted the n-word to be removed from literature because "that word makes me feel uncomfortable and makes me want to throw the book in a pit of fire and dance on the ashes!" Baker concluded that, as an educator, she must continue to have these discussions with her students so that they are not silenced but rather are encouraged to speak up, share their insights and emotions about the power of words, and debate their use.

Frazier (2012) described a similar conversation at an event in New York called "Race Issues in Mark Twain: A Community Dialogue on Language & Dialect in 'Tom Sawyer' and 'Huckleberry Finn,'" sponsored by the National Endowment for the Arts as part of the Big Read program. Over 60 people attended this event, and before long the n-word became the central topic of discussion. "During the entire two-hour conversation," Frazier reported, "almost nothing from either 'Tom Sawyer' or 'Huckleberry Finn' was discussed, except the word" (para. 3). One of the participants, a 10th-grade English teacher, reported that she "lets her students say the word or skip over it, as they prefer, when they read Twain out loud. 'We're never supposed to stop feeling uncomfortable about the word, and that's O.K,'" (para. 3).

In Box 4.8 on pp. 96–97, a high school English teacher describes a project he led with students on the n-word. In his previous vignette in Chapter 3 (Box 3.6 on pp. 63–64), this educator discussed the importance of teaching about the n-word with others in his school and community. His academic rationale for conducting the project is included here, along with highlights from his curriculum, so that other educators can consider how they might teach a curriculum or unit on controversial language.

Names and labels, including terms for self-reference, such as *colored*, *Negro*, and *redneck*, can also be considered controversial language. In *To Kill a Mockingbird*, the use of *Negro* where today we might use *African American* reflects the time period in which the novel was written. But because this label is used in the novel alongside stereotypical or disparaging representations of African Americans, the term *Negro* can be a linguistic microaggression when it is heard or read in contemporary culture. Consider when Scout recalled, "The warm bittersweet smell of clean Negro welcomed us as we entered the churchyard." For contemporary students, the reference to "clean Negro" may be very off-putting, and the label *Negro* may evoke negative impressions for them as a result. African American students in particular may view this type of passage more negatively compared to other students, who may not see themselves reflected in the ethnic labels that are used in the text.

In other situations, the same ethnic label might evoke a positive reaction. A high school English teacher who worked with us described how he incorporates the poetry of Thomas Sayers Ellis into his classroom. He explained that the themes and messages in Ellis's poetry particularly resonate with his Black male students: "One of Ellis's early collections is titled *The Genuine Negro Hero*. I had a student say that he had never seen the words 'Negro' and 'hero' paired in a positive way before."

In a vignette published in *Teaching Tolerance*, Kathryn Knecht (n.d.), a 5th-grade teacher in Illinois, described how she and her students tackled the use of *Negro* and the n-word in literature. When reading *The Cay*, the students encountered the fact that the character Phillip, a blind White boy, calls Timothy, an elderly Black sailor, a Negro. When one African American student suggested that Phillip's use of the term was racist, more than half of the students agreed. To delve deeper into the issue, Knecht and her students investigated the etymology of *Negro* in the dictionary and explored its use during the Jim Crow era. As a homework assignment, the students asked older adults how they felt about the term, collecting answers that ranged from "just fine" to "strictly forbidden." Knecht explained, "The great debate was never completely settled. But every student had given bigotry and labeling serious thought." Ultimately, she and her students concluded that they "should never call anyone what they don't like to be called." Later that

BOX 4.8. AN EDUCATOR'S VIGNETTE: Studying the N-Word: Why and How

Cleveland Winfield,
10th-Grade English and Hip-Hop Verse & Poetry Teacher

As a young African American male English teacher, I feel it is my responsibility to provide my students with an education that exposes them to a range of topics and themes, including those that may be seen as controversial. I recognize the fact that I am a role model, in particular, for African American male students and students of color, and I cannot dodge my duty to address the tough questions they pose to me.

As I designed my curriculum for analyzing the n-word, and as a means of preparing a detailed defense of this endeavor if I were to encounter any resistance, I developed a list of reasons why I believe my students should pursue an in-depth study of the n-word. First, the n-word exists in literature, including the classics *Adventures of Huckleberry Finn*, *To Kill a Mockingbird*, *Their Eyes Were Watching God*, *A Raisin in The Sun*, and "The Man Who Was Almos' a Man." I get asked about the n-word every year, as students are interested in studying it and learning more about how it is used, why it is used, when it is used, and how literature captures and reflects its presence in society.

I believe that students benefit educationally from wrestling with a controversial or taboo term. I want students to be thinkers and not to avoid problems or issues because of scrutiny and/or painful memories and feelings. Studying the n-word helps students know that it is okay to think and question, to venture out into deep water. It helps my students develop their ability to deal with controversial language, topics, and issues and to sharpen their analytical skills. These skills will serve my students well as they move on to advanced classes, including AP and college classes.

My curriculum for the in-depth study of the n-word was centered on interest-driven content. In studying the n-word, I used a mixture of written, audio, and visual texts, which appealed to my students, and I gave them a variety of exercises and assignments.

- Students used prewriting prompts and creative writing exercises to explore their thoughts on the n-word. For example: "How do you feel about the use of the n-word in today's society by Whites, Blacks, in music, in movies, etc.?"
- We studied the various definitions of the terms *nigga* and *nigger,* as well as their variations and spin-off phrases, drawing on Smitherman (2000) as a resource.
- We read and discussed "Like a Winding Sheet," a story by Ann Petry, and "Talk," a poem by Terrance Hayes. We also read and discussed the *Ebony* editorial entitled "Enough!: Why Blacks—and Whites—Should Never Use The 'N-Word' Again," by Bryan Monroe.

- We analyzed the n-word as used by hip-hop artists and Black comedians, including "Mr. Nigga" by Mos Def; "Niggas" by Jhunippuz Elite Poetry Organization; "Nigga Please" by Chris Rock; "Niggatrol" by Chris Rock; "Clayton Bigsby" by Dave Chappelle; and "The Niggar Family" by Dave Chappelle.

Guiding my students in an in-depth analysis of the n-word, I realized that the debate over whether or not African American artists should use the n-word is not a one-time tension that only existed back during the Harlem Renaissance. It is an everyday tension that is still very much part of a heated debate within the African American community. As I shared with my students, reading about the n-word gave me insight into White authors such as Mark Twain who aspired to provide social commentary via their usage of this word. Teaching this course also encouraged me to explore my own thoughts on the use of the word in stand-up comedy routines and in texts and poetry, just as W.E.B. Du Bois and Langston Hughes did in their own literary works.

Although it is a challenging topic, teaching a course on the n-word for the Upward Bound program and a unit with the same focus at my high school has proven to be a rewarding and enlightening experience for me as an educator, as well as for my students. By exploring a controversial term, I have had the privilege of giving my students the opportunity to learn more about various aspects of the racial and linguistic landscape in America.

year, the class read *War Comes to Willy Freeman*, which tells the story of Willy, a young, freed slave girl during the Revolutionary War. The n-word is used frequently in the novel, and students discussed that, although it appears for historical accuracy, they were nevertheless distressed by the word. They decided "that they preferred not to hear the word 'nigger' read out loud," a choice that made Knecht more comfortable as well. Knecht recommended that teachers decide for themselves how to handle controversial language and topics in literature, but she finds no merit in avoidance or censorship, saying, "We cannot ask children to question the meaning of literature if we shelter them from those selections which offer the greatest springboard for thought and discussion."

Each of these examples illustrates the merit of our first linguistic truth: Communication occurs in social contexts. Because communication is complex and nuanced, reflecting our backgrounds, cultures, and identities, language use is often subjective. As parallels to the n-word, students can consider ethnic labels such as *Moor* as used by Shakespeare, *Jew* by Dickens, *white trash* by Flannery O'Connor, and *Indian* by Sherman Alexie. Similarly, secondary English educators and students must decide how to approach words that deal with gender and sexuality, such as *bitch* and *gay*; those that deal with ability, such as *idiot* and *retard*; and swear words, curses, and oaths, which bring issues of religion and morality to the foreground.

Many classic and contemporary works are well known for the liberal use of profanity, including *As I Lay Dying*, *Invisible Man*, *Lord of the Flies*, *Of Mice and Men*, *Slaughterhouse Five*, *The Catcher in the Rye*, *The Color Purple*, *The Grapes of Wrath*, *The Great Gatsby*, and *Ulysses*. Many educators and students feel uncomfortable with profanity, and literature that uses it routinely appears on lists of banned books. Because schools often forbid students and educators from personally using curses, insults, and slurs in order to create a safe and respectful academic environment, it can seem paradoxical to encounter taboo terms in literature read at school. For this reason, it is important for educators to ground a discussion of profanity (and other controversial language) with an explanation of register, which refers to the ways we adjust our language according to a given social situation (see Chapter 2). In school settings, cursing is generally not accepted as part of the academic register, nor is it generally part of the register used in church or at work or in any number of formal settings. In other settings, particularly in informal, everyday contexts, cursing may be acceptable. By discussing register selection, students can analyze the choice of what linguistic forms to use in different contexts and can debate the pros and cons of censorship in literature.

Educators can ground a discussion of controversial language with the fact that there is a long history of the use of slurs, insults, curses, oaths, and swearing in literature and in society in general. The use of taboo language is as old and as widespread as language itself. As Caliban stated to Prospero in *The Tempest*, "You taught me language, and my profit on'tis, I know how to curse." The works of Shakespeare, with their myriad curses, oaths, and insults, provide excellent opportunities for students to examine taboo language through a linguistic and literary lens, focusing on register, language change, and the evolution of English. Students can study how characters use controversial language to express their opposition to conventional attitudes or create distance between themselves and authority. They can also examine how the nature and form of curses, oaths, and insults have changed over time. For instance, some of the strongest oaths in Shakespeare involve swearing by God. *Zounds*, derived from the phrase "God's wounds," was considered at the time to be a vulgar reference to the wounds of Jesus on the cross. Taboo language, like slang, is often at the forefront of language change. Students can therefore analyze taboo language as a case study in how language has evolved. Shakespearean curses and insults often involve gender and sexuality, such as *whoreson* and *bastard*, which parallel curses and insults found in contemporary American English. Other Shakespearean curses and insults would not seem very offensive today. Controversial language can therefore be used as a vehicle to examine language change and its social context, as secondary English educators guide students to build their skills of literary and linguistic analysis.

Because, in life as in literature, language is variable and flexible, there are no easy answers to the question of what controversial language means and how it should be used. Within a framework of linguistically and culturally responsive teaching, secondary English educators can guide students to have respectful conversations about controversial language and other complex and challenging topics. By understanding the nature and context of communication, students can explore how history, society, and culture inform an author's choice—as well as our own—about how to communicate with people who are similar to and different from ourselves.

BECOMING LANGUAGE INVESTIGATORS: ANALYZING THE LANGUAGE OF LITERARY TEXTS

Thus far we have addressed how to approach literary texts that incorporate rich language variation and that give voice to controversial or complex topics. In this section, we discuss how to guide students to become *language investigators* and apply a sociolinguistic lens in order to interpret for themselves the linguistic diversity found in literature. A focus on building students' skills of language investigation aligns with guidelines set by the National Council of Teachers of English (2003), which established the importance of analyzing language as well as literature in the English classroom. As students develop "a better understanding of the nature of language and a greater flexibility and versatility in the choices they make," they are better equipped to "make shifts in tone, style, sentence structure and length, vocabulary, diction, and order" in their own writing (p. 15). Similar assertions are made in the Common Core State Standards for English Language Arts (Common Core State Standards Initiative, 2012b) and by the College Board (2010) in its goals for Advanced Placement English Language and Composition Advanced courses.

To help students become language investigators, educators can encourage students to explore the linguistic context of literary works. One high school English educator explained how she builds her students' awareness of language variation when she teaches texts by Kate Chopin, who "uses a great deal of French Creole language." First, the educator and students discussed French Creole as a language variety—what it looks like, its origins, and its cultural connections—before delving into the literature. "To prepare my students, we discuss the Creole population in New Orleans and the local color movement, and we discuss the characteristics of the Creole community. I also give my students a list of common French Creole words and phrases for their reference." With this background knowledge, she explained, students are better able to understand the language variation that Chopin uses.

It is important to foster students' awareness of and appreciation for language variation, but sometimes students struggle when asked to read a text that includes language variation. To address this challenge, students can listen to or watch performances of the literature. Particularly when nonstandardized spellings are used to represent language variation, hearing a spoken version can help students reconcile the pronunciations with what is printed on the page. Listening to literature can also build familiarity with the language variety and make the literary work more compelling, even for students who do not necessarily find the print version difficult. As one educator who worked with us put it, "I think that any piece of literature becomes transformative when we are allowed to listen to it." For example, one high school English teacher who worked with us uses YouTube clips to reinforce the connection between the spoken and the written word. At first, he said, when he plays a YouTube clip of Thomas Sayers Ellis reciting "All Their Stanzas Look Alike," his students "giggle because of their discomfort with poetry that has true rhythm and feeling." But after they connect the words on the page with the spoken language, "they look at Ellis on the screen and inevitably fall under his spell and begin to play with words in ways they never thought possible. Ellis's works have shown my students the power and the beauty in their own everyday speech." Another high school English educator used this technique in his 11th-grade Honors English class. "One way I teach about language variation is when we read the short story 'Sweat,' by Zora Neale Hurston," he explained. "The dialect is difficult to read, so I have my students listen to the play as well. As a result, we are able to compare the two texts and discuss the similarities and differences in how the language is represented in its spoken and written forms."

With greater awareness of language use and language choice, students are better equipped to conduct close readings of a text. Advanced students can benefit from an in-depth examination of particular linguistic features and how authors use them to portray language variation. One high school English teacher who has worked with us explained that when she teaches Toni Morrison's *The Bluest Eye*, "the novel opens up so many discussions of the beauty of language that it always leads to students' interest in researching language variations and seeing how powerfully these features are involved in storytelling and ethnography." To build this skill, students can select a linguistic feature—such as *ain't*—and explore how it is used for linguistic and literary effect. For example, in the play *A Raisin in the Sun*, there is considerable linguistic variation among the family members. In one scene,

Ruth is trying to get her husband, Walter, and her son, Travis, to finish getting ready in the morning. Walter asks, about Travis, "Ain't he out yet?" Ruth replies, "Out? He ain't hardly got in there good yet." Students can consider how Ruth and Walter use *ain't* and compare and contrast it with the language used by Beneatha, the daughter, who often uses standardized English. Discussion questions that prompt students to conduct a close linguistic analysis include: How does Beneatha's linguistic identity relate to her identity as an African American woman with a formal education, seeking a professional career? What can the single word *ain't* tell us about relationships between characters, about personal identity, and about the role of language in culture and society? Would *A Raisin in the Sun* have had a different effect or meaning if Walter had asked, "Isn't he out yet?" and if Ruth had replied, "Out? He has hardly gotten in"—and if so, how and why? Students can rewrite different literary passages with different linguistic features, tone, register, and audience and discuss how these changes affect meaning, persuasiveness, and emotional appeal.

In addition to *ain't*, a host of other grammar- and sound-related features are commonly used in texts that incorporate language variation (Minnick, 2004). Consider the dialogue in the following passage in *Adventures of Huckleberry Finn*, when Huck first sneaks up on Jim: "We went tiptoeing along a path amongst the trees back towards the end of the widow's garden, stooping down so as the branches wouldn't scrape our heads. When we was passing by the kitchen I fell over a root and made a noise. . . . Then he [Jim] says: 'Who dah?'" In this passage, Huck uses the regularized verb form *was* for *were* ("When we was passing by the kitchen"). Jim's speech includes the deletion of the helping or linking form of the verb *to be* (*Who* instead of *Who is* or *Who's*) as well as the deletion of the *r* sound (*dah* for *there*). Minnick (2004) listed other nonstandardized English features that are found in *Adventures of Huckleberry Finn*:

- completive *done,* as in "She done broke loose"
- plural *-s* absence, as in "Not if it's forty year!"
- *a*-prefixing, as in "I see a light a-comin'"
- multiple negation, as in "He hain't got no family"
- alternations in the *th* sound, as in *sumf'n* for *something*
- consonant cluster reduction, as in *ole* for *old*
- the regularization of past-tense verbs, as in "I knowed"

These grammar- and sound-related features, discussed thoroughly in Charity Hudley and Mallinson (2011), are common in Southern, Appalachian, and African American linguistic and literary traditions. The investigation of the use and meaning of language variation can lead into an exercise in which

BOX 4.9. AN EDUCATOR'S VIGNETTE: Language Variation in *The Wire*

Mario Zangla,
AP English Teacher

I try to bring my own appreciation of the vastness and richness of the English language to my AP Literature students by presenting them with a 2-minute scene from the acclaimed HBO series *The Wire*, where convicted felons sit in a prison library discussing Fitzgerald's *The Great Gatsby*. The English teachers of my youth (and more than a few of my present colleagues) would probably be appalled by the liberal use of colloquialisms and nonstandard English in this scene. Subjects and verbs frequently disagree, tenses are misused, and verbs are sometimes dropped altogether. The use of phrases such as *best not*, *he frontin'*, *he ain't read nary one of them*, and *'cuz he wasn't ready to get real with the story* might also cause some alarm in a traditional English classroom.

But as a teacher in a school that has many "nontraditional" AP students, I use these 2 minutes of what some might view as "butchered" English to broaden my students' minds as to what constitutes literary analysis. When the teacher states, "Fitzgerald said that there are no second acts in American lives. Do you believe that?" he is posing an essay prompt to the group. When the character D'Angelo responds with, "The past is always with us—where we came from, what we go through, how we go through it," he is stating an assertion for a paragraph of analysis. When the teacher prompts him with "Go ahead," D'Angelo provides relevant commentary and textual citations that develop his assertion.

The effect of this exercise is that my students learn the structure of an analytical argument in the least intimidating manner possible. The language variations used by D'Angelo and his fellow inmates are something my students are used to in their everyday lives, but it is often alien to an AP English classroom. The fact that their teacher would use this scene as a positive model for what constitutes analytical discussion allows my students to use the language they are most comfortable with, which helps free up their minds for analysis.

Later in the year we encounter characters such as Pilate (from *Song of Solomon*), the Gravedigger (from *Hamlet*), and Job (from *The Sound and the Fury*). I ask my students to analyze how these characters, despite speaking in traditionally denigrated language varieties, compete with, and sometimes outwit, their supposed superiors. They can engage in this task because they have learned to tease out the value in all language. Like D'Angelo says, they are "ready to get real with the story."

students compile linguistic profiles of characters—a parallel to an exercise in which students create psychological profiles of characters (Gibbons, 2009). As students explore the ways that linguistic elements—such as regional phrases, idioms, metaphor, and the names and nicknames of characters—contribute meaning and style to a text, they can consider whether they use similar or different linguistic elements in their own speech and writing, with what intention, and to what effect. Each of these tasks builds students' awareness of linguistic choice, register, style, and tone, with regard to other authors as well as themselves as speakers and writers.

CONCLUSION

There are tangible benefits for students who engage with literary language. Language gives us insight into literary characters as well as ourselves. Seen through a linguistic lens, literature can reveal societal attitudes about different groups of people and the language they speak. Literature can also be a touchstone for helping students explore many of the themes we have covered throughout this book, including communicative competence, representation, naming, and labeling. Students can learn the value of varied modes of expression and how literature can be a vehicle for authors to speak up, speak out, and challenge social conventions. With these understandings, students can make text-to-self connections in ways that help build their skills of speaking and writing, in ways that express their identities and establish their voice.

Within a framework of linguistically and culturally responsive education, secondary English educators can instruct students about the power of language and the linguistic value of diverse literary texts. Language can both free us and bind us, and as students are taught to harness the power of language themselves, they can gain the confidence to bridge the gap between literary worlds and their own and seek to add their voices to the literary canon. With this theme in mind, we turn to Chapter 5, in which we examine the role and relevance of language in students' own narratives, particularly in the transition from secondary settings to college.

CHAPTER 5

Doing Language: The Transition to College and Beyond

As SECONDARY STUDENTS TRANSITION from high school into college and careers, they become scholars in their own right, with their own voices and stories to tell. In this chapter, we discuss how secondary English educators can help students "do language" (Morrison, 1993) in ways that will prepare them to transition from secondary to postsecondary settings. We examine how secondary English educators can guide students to develop the communication skills they need, both to meet the complex and varied linguistic expectations of college and to add their voice and perspective to the academic discourse. As part of this process, students must learn to transfer their everyday reading and writing skills to academic contexts, which is a challenge for many students. Through strategies and concepts presented in this chapter, we explore how secondary English educators can help students develop a strong and compelling narrative voice, balancing language that is true to themselves with language that is easily understood by others.

The skills we center on in this chapter are not only valuable for students who want to study literature in college or become scholars of the English language. The transition to college is a focus of major state and federal initiatives (Brandon, 2009), and language is a central factor in student preparation and student success in higher education. Our work has shown us the critical importance of strengthening the communication skills of culturally and linguistically diverse students from underrepresented groups who may be prepared enough to be competent in college but who may need additional preparation to excel. At our universities and in collaboration with organizations such as Middle Grades Partnership in Baltimore, Maryland, and the School-University Research Network (SURN) in Williamsburg, Virginia, we work with students from underrepresented groups to help them succeed in postsecondary environments, often by partnering with the secondary educators who helped these students get to college and who want to see them graduate with more than basic proficiency. Quotes and vignettes from secondary English educators who have participated in these and other partnerships speak to the importance of language in helping culturally and linguistically diverse students develop the skills they need to succeed after high school.

DEVELOPING STUDENTS' LINGUISTIC AGENCY

Students who are not prepared for the linguistic expectations of college and career settings are at a distinct disadvantage. This sentiment has been echoed by many educators who have worked with us. "I attended a workshop on critical thinking that included teachers from middle, high school, community college, and universities," one secondary English educator said. "The topic they presented, and that is still being discussed via discussion board, is the disconnect between high school and college—in other words, how our students are not prepared for the level of critical thinking and rigor involved at the college level." To most effectively and efficiently help students transition from high school to college settings, more information must be shared about how communication skills are valued and evaluated in postsecondary environments.

In college environments, communication tends to be conceptualized broadly. For example, college-level writing instruction often centers on building students' competence in critical argumentation, while proficiency with the mechanics of standardized English may be assumed. As the phrase "writing across the curriculum" attests, a great deal of attention is paid to helping students consider how to communicate with a variety of audiences and choose appropriate modes of communication for specific communicative tasks. In addition to writing skills, the skills of rhetoric and public speaking are similarly emphasized for college students, no matter if they are communications majors or—as we have learned from our own research into the language of STEM classrooms (Mallinson & Charity Hudley, 2011; forthcoming)—biology, physics, or math majors. To be successful, all students must develop strong oral communication skills, including how to ask questions, interact as part of diverse groups, seek faculty guidance, and effectively present their research.

In the following sections, we explore how secondary English educators can help students develop their communication skills in ways that benefit students as they transition from secondary English classrooms to postsecondary environments. Just as in Chapter 4, where we promoted the concept of guiding students to become language investigators when they study literature, we set a similar goal with regard to the language of higher education and, by extension, other professional settings. Secondary English educators are well positioned to help students understand the importance of language as it is used in their everyday lives. As students develop the linguistic flexibility and versatility to communicate in varied professional environments, they develop important literacy skills and linguistic agency.

Talking College and Community

Although pre-collegiate students often envision a college or university as a place where largely passive learning takes place within big lecture halls, the language of higher education is not confined to this format. Communicating in classrooms is central, but students also must be prepared for the language of the broad college experience, which includes meeting with financial aid officers, speaking with advisors, attending office hours, and drafting emails to faculty, staff, employers, and other students. The linguistic expectations that govern these interactions are often thought of as nothing more than basic politeness or common sense. Verbal skills that are often considered polite or part of common knowledge may rest on cultural assumptions and unspoken modes of communication, however. We take the position that norms and expectations about what counts as polite and appropriate communication must be explicitly talked about and explicitly taught to students by teachers and mentors. By demystifying and clarifying the process of how to interact in higher education environments, educators can promote the college readiness of all their students, not only those who have prior knowledge of or familiarity with the conventions of academic communication.

In college, students meet faculty and staff who, at least at the beginning of a student's college career, are strangers. Many students, for the first time in their lives, will need to depend on strangers, not only for grades and advice but for housing, food, finances, and countless other services. And many of these strangers will expect that students know the protocols for appropriate college communication, often from day one. It is not the case that communication in college settings is rigid or sanitized but rather that certain linguistic norms have developed, as in any professional setting. Before we discuss what some of those expectations are, we explain one point that is important for secondary English educators to impart to their college-bound students above any other: the importance of asking questions and seeking advice—to speak up in order to learn. Even though faculty and staff expect students to communicate in ways that follow certain conventions, almost everyone will welcome students' inquiries about how to correspond and even about what are good questions to ask when the student doesn't know where to begin.

Students who don't ask when they need help or information can face unfortunate consequences. In a recent survey of 70 college students (Dickter & Charity Hudley, 2013), those who said that they felt unsupported during college also said that they had felt too intimidated to ask questions, didn't know where to seek out answers, and didn't feel that they had the extra time to talk to faculty. Students who feel unsupported are also more likely to have a negative college experience or to drop out. Fortunately, the opposite is also true: Students who speak up, ask questions when they don't understand, make connections with faculty and staff, and get engaged in campus life are more likely to have a positive college experience. Rather than waiting for opportunities to present themselves or for answers to unasked questions to materialize, students must take the initiative to seek out what they need to succeed. It is particularly important for students from backgrounds that have been traditionally underrepresented and underserved in higher education, whose families and friends may have less prior experience with college protocols, to understand the significance of asking. The idea that unarticulated linguistic expectations operate in college environments may seem especially daunting for these students and for the educators who are preparing them to make this transition. It is important to remember that these norms need not and should not be left unspoken. Box 5.1 on pp. 108–109 provides an adaptation of Anne's orientation addresses to the College of William & Mary Classes of 2016 and 2017. She discusses some of the linguistic and cultural expectations for college, but she also asserts that it is always important to *ask*. For this reason, learning to ask must be part of college instruction. Materials such as Anne's vignette can be shared with college-bound students to help them prepare for higher education and understand how communication is central to college life.

The primary reason that we discuss the linguistic expectations of college is not to suggest that professors are overly concerned with propriety or that colleges want to dictate how students should talk and behave. Rather, through open and explicit discussion of communicative norms, we aim to level the linguistic playing field for college-bound students. As we have mentioned, students who come to college already familiar with the ways that professors and students are expected to communicate are at an advantage over those who don't have this linguistic know-how. Unless the norms of college communication are clearly taught to all students before they get to college, students from underserved backgrounds—students who may not learn this information at home, students who may say things differently in their communities—may have to work harder to have their voices heard. And, of course, not all students will be able to navigate this added challenge, nor should they have to. Secondary educators who can explain norms about how to communicate in college and clarify protocols that can sometimes feel mysterious or idiosyncratic therefore can help promote the college readiness of all their students.

Some of the communicative expectations that are often left unarticulated in higher education involve linguistic features we discussed in this book,

BOX 5.1. A SOCIOLINGUIST'S VIGNETTE: The Importance of Asking Questions

Dr. Anne H. Charity Hudley,
Associate Professor of Education, English, Linguistics, and Africana Studies and the William & Mary Professor of Community Studies at the College of William & Mary

Welcome to the College of William & Mary! I've been asked to talk to you today about classroom and academic expectations. In short, we expect you to be scholars. What does it mean to be a scholar? It means you get to ask yourselves and then, more importantly, answer the following questions.

First, how many more lives can you touch as a college educated person, including your own? You are now living your dream. Yesterday, I spoke with students who were third-generation William & Mary students, and I spoke with students who were the first in their families to go to college. What an amazing range of legacy and new spirits we are combining here, working within a liberal arts framework for a public good.

Second, how much good you can do for the world, and what can you contribute both to your local community and the world at large? Good can be defined in many ways—intellectually, financially, socially, and spiritually, to name just a few. We wait to see what ideas you will create, what models you will build, and what solutions you will discover. Learning content is just the beginning; synthesizing it and building upon it is the name of the game. We are here to be masters of knowledge. We are also here to challenge the status quo and to be full-time thinkers and dreamers!

To make this type of scholarship possible it is important to think about some of the possible differences between your high school experiences and the experiences that you will have in college. In high school, school or state standards determined much of what you had to know. In college, in many ways, you will decide what you need to know. Individual professors working with general college and state guidelines also will determine what you need to know.

It is therefore important to understand the expectations of individual professors, and the only way to know is to ask. That means asking about things big and small, especially because small things may end up to be big. Ask what the professor wishes to be called both in person and on email. Some prefer *Professor*, some prefer *Dr.* if they hold a doctorate (ask if they do), some prefer *Ms.* or *Mrs.* or *Miss*, and others prefer to be called by their first name (again, ask!). Ask all professors about their policies and philosophies on the use of laptops and phones. Professors have different rules and it's important to understand their rationales. I take notes on my iPhone, but to other professors that might appear as if you are not engaged and are texting, so you need to know what they expect. If plagiarism has been explained to you, but you are still unsure of all that it entails, ask! If there is something you want to know that hasn't been explained yet, ask!

In high school, you most often studied according to a predetermined program and schedule. Here at William & Mary, you can study and research whatever you are interested in. We are here to make it happen together! For those reasons, it's important to work with professors both inside and outside of the classroom so that you can best understand what is expected of you. Many of us teach classes and direct research groups or labs, and our strongest students often find their ways into both. I'll also put a plug in here for self-designed majors and minors that let you combine your interests in innovative ways.

It is up to you to ensure that your readings and practice problems and exercises are completed before class. It is up to you to make sure that you understand the syllabus and the information provided. It is up to you to make sure you have all that you need to succeed and that we have all the information we need to help you. It is up to you to make sure that we as faculty understand what your definition of success is and that you understand our definitions as well. So ask!

such as the use of honorifics and abbreviations. They also include features of standardized English that we discussed in Charity Hudley and Mallinson (2011), such as sentence structure, vocabulary, and tone. Other linguistic expectations of college environments intersect with professional norms of politeness, which include how to thank the person on the other end of the phone or email exchange and whether or not to do so (as we discuss in Box 5.2 on pp. 110–111, the answer is yes!). Linguistic tips for college abound in books and online (Johnson, 2012; WikiHow, n.d.), and this advice also applies to students and colleagues in post-collegiate environments. For example, Patton (2012) reported the views of faculty from various colleges and universities about how they prefer students and other colleagues to address them, particularly via email.

As we stated earlier, while questions such as how to write an email with appropriate tone and how to use honorifics are often viewed as being a matter of respect and professionalism, we are not advocating that these norms need to be followed for reasons of mere propriety. Rather, the goal of teaching students about which conventions operate in which settings and how to follow them if they choose is part of a larger pedagogical strategy of giving students the tools they need to be able to help themselves. The linguistic playing field is leveled when all students' voices are given the attention and respect in college environments that they deserve, irrespective of the linguistic conventions that the students knew or didn't know when they first arrived on campus.

Simply providing students with information about the linguistic expectations of college often isn't enough; students have to understand the norms and practice the skills required to adhere to them. Secondary English educators can help habituate students to ways of communicating in post-

BOX 5.2. A SOCIOLINGUIST'S VIGNETTE: The Linguistic Expectations of College Communication

Dr. Christine Mallinson,
Associate Professor of Language, Literacy, and Culture at the University of Maryland–Baltimore County

Students who understand the linguistic expectations of college will be at an advantage when they operate in postsecondary environments. For this reason, it is important for all educators, and particularly secondary English educators, to explicitly teach these norms and conventions to all students—and especially to students who have less experience with the type of professional communication that is valued in college settings—so that they arrive on college campuses fully prepared to speak up and have their voices heard and respected. Here are five simple but important tips that I developed when tutoring high school students in Baltimore to teach them about the linguistic expectations of college. Secondary English educators can instruct students on these items and encourage students to practice each of them, well before they set foot on campus.

First, use honorifics. At the beginning of every communication, always use *Dr.* or *Professor* plus the person's last name (e.g., *Dr. Smith*, not *Dr. Marie*) to address the faculty member on the other end of the phone or the email exchange. Similarly, use *Mr.* or *Ms.* with staff. These honorifics should always be used unless faculty or staff members request otherwise. Only after other people say, "Please, call me by my first name," or use their first name in their responses is it okay to do so as well. On many campuses, staff members also have doctorates, and the use of *Dr.* is also appropriate for them.

Second, complete sentences are a must. Also, in an email, sentences should not come in a long string, one after the other; a large block of text is difficult for any reader to parse. Instead, use paragraph breaks and indentation to separate each different thought into chunks. Finally, even though emails allow for instantaneous communication, they should nevertheless be thought out and revised to be as clear as possible. Emails should be reread, or (even better) read out loud, to be certain they make sense before hitting "send."

Third, abbreviations (other than in honorifics such as *Dr.*) should be avoided entirely. Abbreviations are shortcuts without a payoff: they can be confusing for people who don't know what they mean, they can easily be mistyped, and they can be misread. Type out everything fully, at least in the first email or letter. In follow-up writing, common abbreviations can be used, but sparingly. Abbreviations that are part of texting language should never be used as part of college communication with faculty and staff, unless they use them first.

Fourth, in any email or phone conversation, providing context and background information is critical. Faculty and staff receive hundreds of emails every day, often from students they don't know well and possibly have never met. For this reason, it is important to explain fully who the student is, what is being asked, to give relevant details, and to provide enough background information so that the other person doesn't have to struggle to figure out what is being referred to. For instance, when inquiring about homework, include the name of the professor's course, the date, and the homework topic in question. Professors teach many courses, and they don't always remember which student is which. Similarly, when communicating with the registrar, for instance, important identifying details might include one's full name and student number.

Fifth, and finally, express gratitude. *Every* correspondence, whether oral or written, should include a thank you to the person on the other end of the exchange. Even when the subject matter of the correspondence is tense—such as when contesting something that a student doesn't think is fair—a statement of gratitude at the beginning and the end of the exchange will improve the likelihood that the message is heard and the messenger is respected. It is difficult to overestimate the many demands that are placed on faculty and staff to respond to students, and every query takes time to answer. For this reason, it is important to always say thanks. These linguistic niceties will always be appreciated.

secondary environments by giving them opportunities to become familiar with these styles. Students can write skits or participate in role-playing activities in which they imagine being on a college campus, in a specific setting, and carrying out a specific task, such as setting up an appointment with the registrar. What office should they contact? Should they call or email? What should they say? What happens next? Students can be given real-life assignments, such as emailing, calling, or visiting a faculty or a staff member at a local college (preferably one that the educator has contacted in advance) to ask a question. They can also visit a college library and ask for help with tasks such as understanding how to find a book or a journal and how to search catalogs and databases. These assignments give students authentic opportunities to hone their professional academic communication skills, and students may be more motivated to learn this information as they see firsthand the relevance of these tasks.

Secondary English educators can also learn about the linguistic expectations of college and give their students opportunities to practice the skills they need to know by building bridges between secondary and postsecondary environments. Through opportunities such as school-university partnerships and professional development schools, secondary English educators can learn from college professors what communication skills their high school students need to know in order to succeed in postsecondary environments. Similarly, to provide the best instruction at the college level, all professors, especially English professors, need to know what their students learned in high school and be aware of students' linguistic backgrounds (Behrens, 2012; Williams, 2012). Professors and staff are also in a position to provide support and be role models for college students who speak nonstandardized varieties of English and who may face language-related challenges in higher education settings (Dunstan, 2013).

Service-learning initiatives, which are increasingly part of students' postsecondary learning experiences (Wurr & Hellebrandt, 2007), can also facilitate partnerships across high school and college lines. Secondary students benefit from these opportunities by being exposed to dimensions of college life and learning, college students benefit from the chance to mentor and give back, and secondary and postsecondary educators can share with and learn from each other. At the College of William & Mary and at UMBC, we both teach service-learning courses. In Anne's course, college students partnered with a special school for middle and high school students who had been suspended or expelled from the general public school population (Charity et al., 2008). These college students were able to mentor the middle and high school students and provide them with support, using the lessons that they themselves had so recently learned and lived. In Christine's course, students interned with high school educators to codesign educational projects on language and culture. In both seminars, students discussed the relationship between language, culture, and education, while at their service-learning sites, they witnessed the importance of mentorship and collaboration and explored the complexities of language in real-world settings. Service-learning also teaches students about professionalism. In order to serve, they must partner with others, communicating with diverse groups and working together in teams. The writing and speaking skills that students use in service-learning experiences are not abstract but rather audience-specific and purpose-driven, which helps foster linguistic awareness and flexibility. In service-learning situations and in other forms of engagement, communication is central.

Service-learning experiences can also connect the multiple audiences who are central to the message of our book, bringing secondary English educators and students together with faculty and students from colleges and universities. In an illustration of this model, Sara Brandt, who teaches senior-level general and AP English, participated in the 2011 Capstone English Academy in Virginia. One of her goals as a high school English educator was to foster her students' college readiness by exposing them to a college environment. Sara partnered with professors at the College of William & Mary to plan service-learning experiences that would benefit the college students as well as the high school students. She brought 12 students to tour campus, meet students and professors, and attend a class in which professors talked to them about the expectations of college, and college students talked about their experiences. Later that year, the college students visited Sara's high school class, where they helped students complete their final multimedia projects. Through this service-learning experience, bridges were built among secondary and postsecondary students and educators, as well as between secondary and postsecondary institutions.

Service-learning opportunities can also be designed that bring high school students and college students together to conduct research, broadening the real-world and academic skills of both groups. As seen in Box 5.3, sociolinguist and professor Dr. Mary Bucholtz founded an innovative community-based program, School Kids Investigating Language in Life and Society, or SKILLS. The SKILLS program is a partnership that brings together traditionally underserved high school students in Santa Barbara County with high school educators, college students, graduate students, and professors at the University of California, Santa Barbara. As the teams of students and faculty conduct authentic research, students build their skills of data collection and analysis as well as collaboration and teamwork. In addition, the high school educators and the professors make connections across academic institutions, while the high school students receive mentorship that guides them toward college by providing concrete strategies and pathways for success.

BOX 5.3. A SOCIOLINGUIST'S VIGNETTE: Teaching Students the SKILLS of Linguistic Research

Dr. Mary Bucholtz,
Professor of Linguistics at the University of California, Santa Barbara

The SKILLS program (www.skills.ucsb.edu) is founded on a simple principle: Young people have a wealth of linguistic and cultural expertise that is typically not used, valued, or even recognized in traditional schooling. This expertise can include knowledge of the latest youth slang, the linguistic flexibility of bilingualism and bidialectalism, and the ability to use language effectively to carry out a range of cultural activities in peer group, family, and community settings. SKILLS was created in the belief that students benefit both academically and personally by gaining awareness and appreciation of their own and others' linguistic expertise. The program acknowledges students as linguistic experts by guiding them through the process of carrying out original empirical research on language and culture in their lives. These experiences in turn provide a strong foundation for student-researchers to develop their academic skills as well as their collegiate identities, as they come to realize the value of their linguistic expertise and the excitement and rewards of contributing to the making of new knowledge through research. By forging partnerships with high schools and academic preparation programs such as Upward Bound and AVID, the SKILLS program creates collaborations among university professors, high school teachers, and graduate, undergraduate, and high school students in which everyone is both a learner and an expert.

SKILLS brings graduate students with linguistics training into local high school settings, where they collaborate with high school teachers to develop and implement an inquiry-based curriculum. SKILLS provides a complete curriculum as a starting point, but the teaching team is encouraged to adapt the course structure and content to fit the needs of each school and the interests and expertise of the instructors. As a result, the SKILLS program has been structured in a variety of ways since it was established in 2010:

- A 20-week technology-rich elective social studies class for 15 to 20 Latino/a and Anglo juniors and seniors in a small rural high school
- A weekly after-school enrichment program for a dozen Latino/a sophomores focused on recognizing and challenging linguistic discrimination
- A 3-day-a-week component of a sophomore-level AVID class for over 35 Latino/a and African American students in a large urban school
- A year-long class for approximately 80 Latino/a and African American first-year students through seniors from five high schools throughout the county as part of Upward Bound's Saturday College program on the University of California, Santa Barbara (UCSB) campus

Thanks to a partnership with Santa Barbara City College, a local community college, students in some versions of SKILLS are able to earn college credit for their participation. At the end of the program, the SKILLS student-researchers come to UCSB to share the results of their work with an audience of university faculty and students, school officials, family members, and members of the general public. These presentations are often the first time in their lives that students experience themselves as respected authorities interacting with adults in an academic setting. Their research is also shared with a wider public through the SKILLS website, which also provides curricular materials and university-based research that has emerged from the program.

SKILLS primarily serves public high school students in Santa Barbara County, a population that is largely Latino/a, working-class, and first-generation college-bound. We especially aim to support students who are high-aspiring but need additional mentoring and academic preparation to achieve their educational goals. However, the curriculum is designed to be flexible enough to reach students of all linguistic, ethnoracial, socioeconomic, and academic backgrounds. A key goal of the program is to help all students, including those who think they "don't have a culture" or lack any noteworthy linguistic expertise, to realize that nearly all Americans, regardless of background, share a history of linguistic discrimination and language shift due to the rigid language ideologies that have always dominated U.S. culture. At the same time, the program helps students to discover the linguistic flexibility and creativity in the speech of their friends, family, and community members, and to recognize this resource as valuable and even powerful. By focusing on spoken language, SKILLS also fosters students' appreciation of the full range of human linguistic capabilities and complements the emphasis on written language and prescriptive grammar that students encounter in other classes.

In its fullest form, the SKILLS curriculum systematically moves students from an examination of language in their peer groups to language in their families, to language in their local communities, to language in the wider world. The curriculum combines interactive multimedia lectures, in-class discussions and hands-on activities, and step-by-step development of original research projects. The first unit, which focuses on the peer group, introduces the student-researchers to basic linguistic concepts and methods by guiding them through the process of contributing to an online slang dictionary hosted on the SKILLS website, for which they collect and analyze audio recordings of the slang terms that they and their friends use in ordinary conversation. In the second unit, the student-researchers turn their focus to language in the family by conducting an oral history with a family elder on the role of language in their lives, an experience that helps solidify understanding of sociolinguistic phenomena like language shift and also allows students to learn more about members of their own family. In the third unit, the student-researchers form teams and conduct an ethnographic study of language and culture in a local community setting, such as a church, organization, or business; they collect and analyze linguistic and cultural data from fieldnotes, video recordings, and interviews with community members.

The experience of carrying out original research has lasting benefits both for students themselves, as they move toward college, and for the university partners. The data that the student-researchers collect is housed in an archive at UCSB's Center for California Languages and Cultures, where it becomes a resource for further research by faculty, graduate students, and undergraduates. In addition, video recordings of classroom activities and an archive of students' classwork and journal writing help us identify which aspects of the program are most effective and which areas need revision.

In short, SKILLS student-researchers gain a great deal from their participation in the program. Not only do they build on their existing linguistic expertise to acquire important academic skills but they also undergo the transformative experience of appreciating the crucial role of language in their own and others' lives. In addition, as producers of original research they are able to witness firsthand the impact of their work as scholars in shaping and transforming our knowledge of language and culture.

Speak Up and Write, Blog, Text, Tweet

In addition to the fact that college-bound students need strong oral communication skills in order to succeed in college environments, they increasingly need to be competent in the use of new literacies, or what the National Council of Teachers of English has called "21st-century literacies" (James R. Squire Office of Policy Research, 2007). The call for students to be capable digital writers is upheld by many organizations who set forth English language standards, including the National Council of Teachers of English and the International Reading Association (1996) and the Common Core State Standards Initiative (2012c), and in the standards for Advanced Placement English Language and Composition courses (College Board, 2010). Many of these standards align with a New Literacy Studies approach, which recognizes that language and literacy development is a social practice and that communication is inherently multimodal (Gee, 1996; Kress, 2003).

Technology is increasingly relevant to multimodal communication. We use gestures along with words when we speak, and we rely on visual images, from the letters on the keyboard and their representation on the screen when we type to the emoticons that many writers use. In college, students are encouraged to view communication as flexible, variable, audience- and genre-specific, and multimodal. Although traditional research papers and literacy practices are still important in higher education, professors are increasingly incorporating technology into their teaching. In many college English classrooms (and in many college classrooms in general), students are expected to theorize the role of new literacies in society, tailor their own communication to specific audiences and for specific aims, engage in digital writing, and create multimodal texts, such as short films, digital stories, and podcasts (Banks, 2011). In 2012, at the College of William & Mary, three college English professors, including Anne, held a roundtable discussion to share how they integrate audiovisual materials into English, Film Studies, and Linguistics courses. They discussed how today's students have "easy and efficient access to media," including video- and image-sharing sites such as YouTube and Flickr, which can lead to more student-centered teaching by enabling students to "contribute examples of texts and media to their courses" (Lawrence, 2012).

In 2012, undergraduate and graduate students in Christine's course "Language in Diverse Schools and Communities" created 45-minute podcasts on language in and around Baltimore for use in high school and college classrooms. Students worked in teams to create podcasts, which are permanently housed on a course blog (Mallinson, 2011). Multimodal projects are not simply creative; they also benefit students' research and writing skills. For example, creating a podcast requires students to select a topic, interview respondents, write a script, edit text and sound, and work in teams. As a student who created one of the Baltimore language podcasts put it, "I became more engaged in the learning through constructing knowledge rather than simply receiving it. . . . Instead of using the technology to merely deliver content, . . . we were given high levels of agency, and the processes of teamwork, dialogue and progressive problem solving were encouraged" (Mallinson, 2011). In Box 5.4 on p. 117, a secondary English educator who worked with us discussed how she used podcasts in her classroom.

BOX 5.4. AN EDUCATOR'S VIGNETTE: Creating Podcasts to Make Students' Ideas Resonate

Kerrigan Mahoney,
Doctoral Student in Education at the College of William & Mary and Former High School English Educator

A blank piece of paper can be an overwhelming obstacle for many students. Tone, mood, and imagery often do not resonate with all students as they read and write. By creating a podcast, students utilize tangible strategies with sound effects, music, and their own voices to communicate their ideas.

To help students see the value in their words, to consider their words critically, and to reflect on the differences between speaking and writing, I have had my students use podcasts. The steps to creating a podcast have parallels in the writing process. The podcast itself can be the final product but can also be used as a jumping off point for transforming the audio into a written essay. The organization of the podcast can parallel the traditional essay, with multiple paragraphs and sections, thesis statement, supporting evidence, and analysis, or it can follow a more organic pattern.

When creating their podcasts, students make stylistic choices based on a consideration of how best to communicate their ideas, which allows for a focus on audience and voice. Students actually hear their own voices and learn how they sound to other people. Sharing the podcasts with an audience is essential. When students know that their voices will be heard by their peers, there is an additional incentive to think about how to communicate effectively. The power of a live audience is concrete for students in a way that handing in a paper that only a teacher is going to read is often not. Through podcasts, the individual voice of each student is given weight and is allowed to resonate.

As students developed content to be read by someone other than just their instructor, they found the task more relevant and were more motivated to engage in the task at hand. The skills that are cultivated through these types of activities are valued in English Language Arts standards, in college and graduate school settings, and in career settings, as employers increasingly look for employees with digital literacy skills, social media savvy, and the ability to collaborate and network online (Preston, 2012).

Information and communication technologies (such as texting, blogs, wikis, podcasts, and digital stories), social network sites (such as Facebook and Twitter), video-sharing sites (such as YouTube), and image-sharing sites (such as Tumblr, Pinterest, and Instagram) can be powerful teaching tools that help prime today's secondary English students to speak and write in ways that also prepare them for college settings. Students can uncover the communicative value of new literacy practices, exploring where the conventions of the spoken and the written word intersect as well as where they differ. For example, students can debate the following issues: Is written language the template for spoken language, is spoken language the template for written language, or is it neither, or both? In what situations is writing of primary importance, as opposed to oral communication? In what circumstances it is valuable to be concise, and when is exposition best? When talking to students about the differences across various types of language—oral language, written language, or genres like texting that lie somewhere in between, educators can also take the opportunity to discuss, as a parallel, how students can balance the use of standardized and nonstandardized varieties of English in their own everyday communication. As such, students can be guided to develop their traditional literacy skills alongside their new literacy skills.

As we discussed in Chapter 2, language differences are natural and normal, and language—including the language our students use—is always changing and variable. In line with these linguistic truths, students can be encouraged to feel pride in the fact that they, too, are actors in the evolution of the English language and that they are speakers with authentic voices who have their own literature to write. As summarized by Lapp, Fisher, and Frey (2012), "[W]e are intent on not missing the opportunity to use all of these [21st-century literacy] resources to support students as they gain control of their grammar, writing conventions, and writing within and across genres" (p. 8). By guiding students to study their use of language in everyday settings and contexts, secondary English educators acknowledge where students are starting from and harness their linguistic innovation as a tool in developing their communicative talents (Morrell, Dueñas, Garcia, & López, 2013).

Creativity in the secondary English classroom, which can include the use of new literacies, does not hinder communication or the development of literacy skills but rather can foster them. The use of personally relevant topics and real-world writing assignments, especially those that incorporate technology, can help students write about something they find important, which benefits all students, but particularly students who may feel less invested in communicating through traditional means alone. Technology is a powerful tool for encouraging students to communicate, and students who are familiar with digital writing and who are practiced users of technology will be able to capitalize on these skills in college. By providing tools that encourage the development of literacy, language awareness, and self-expression, secondary English educators can help ensure that all students—not just those who come to school with a strong ability to use standardized English—are given platforms to speak up and speak out.

BOX 5.5. CURRICULAR CONNECTIONS:
Using Twitter and Texting to Teach Poetic Form

Different genres of poetry operate according to different formal restrictions. For example, sonnets typically contain 14 lines and follow a particular rhyme scheme; they also often follow a regular meter. The traditional Japanese poetic form known as haiku consists of 17 sound units that are roughly equivalent to syllables in English, often expressed in phrases of 5, 7, and 5.

Students can extend their understanding of poetic forms such as the sonnet and haiku by comparing and contrasting them with an analysis of the formal restrictions of Twitter, the microblogging service that allows users to create messages with a 140-character limit. Students can create Twitter sonnets or Twitter haikus to explore the similarities and differences across these genres. As individuals or as a class, students can publish their poems on Twitter and analyze the audience reception they receive. Research has found that the use of Twitter in the classroom is associated with a range of positive outcomes, including improvement of composition skills and development of technological literacy (Black, 2009) as well as higher grades, increased student engagement, and better relationships between students and instructors (Junco, Heiberger, & Loken, 2011).

The poetic form exercise can also be adapted to texting. According to linguist David Crystal (2008), there are many similarities between traditional poetry and poetry written in nontraditional genres, such as via SMS (i.e., via texting):

> The length constraint in text-poetry fosters economy of expression in much the same way as other tightly constrained forms of poetry do, such as the haiku or the Welsh englyn. To say a poem must be written within 160 characters [the limit for most texts] at first seems just as pointless as to say that a poem must be written in three lines of 5, 7, and 5 syllables. But put such a discipline in the hands of a master, and the result can be poetic magic. Of course, SMS poetry has some way to go before it can match the haiku tradition; but then, haikus have had a head-start of several hundred years.

Carol Ann Duffy, the first woman Poet Laureate in Britain, drew similar parallels. Poetry is "a perfecting of a feeling in language—it's a way of saying more with less," she said, "just as texting is." In this regard, the poem can be seen as "a form of texting . . . it's the original text." As Duffy went on to assert, for the "Facebook generation," "poetry is the perfect form for them. It's kind of a time capsule—it allows feelings and ideas to travel big distances in a very condensed form" (Moorhead, 2011).

Exercises that involve Twitter and texting can help engage all students with poetry—those who love poetry already, as well as those who claim they don't understand it or feel that it has little to do with their own lives. By examining how poetry is similar to and different from their own writing, students can become more engaged with the study of poetic form and genre. Secondary English educators who want to take this concept further can also guide students to use short pieces of writing to build toward longer essays. For example, students can text or tweet their reactions for each chapter they read in a novel and use their collection of texts or tweets as notes for writing a longer analytical paper. By working with genres of writing that students are already familiar with and proficient in, secondary English educators can build upon and use students' everyday writing practices as a resource.

THE LANGUAGE AT THE CENTER OF OUR NARRATIVES

The process of encouraging students to develop their linguistic agency can carry forward as students develop their writing skills—especially as they create narrative prose. Narratives are powerful because they express truth that is situated in a writer's point of view. Through the use of voice, speakers and writers employ narratives to communicate perspectives and often to express to others something autobiographical, about who they are and where they come from. In some educational standards, including the Common Core State Standards and Partnership for Assessment of Readiness for College and Careers (PARCC), less emphasis is placed on personal narrative. Yet, in college writing, students are often asked to add their own personal voices to written narratives—and, in doing so, bring their authentic voices to the college experience. Royster (1996) called for embracing a diverse range of authentic voices in educational communities, and she described the intellectual and social challenges that African American women may face when adding their voices to the higher education narrative.

Great authors have mastered the art of storytelling in oral and written forms, and in the secondary English classroom, their texts (and thus, their voices) are often held up as exemplars for students who are learning to craft prose. A common difficulty faced by secondary English educators, however, is how to encourage and guide students to create their own rich and compelling oral and written narratives—narratives that draw upon students' personal experiences while still illustrating broader themes, and narratives that incorporate students' authentic language while still being clear to others. In this section, we explore how secondary English educators can help students balance speaking with power and personality and speaking in an accessible way, which enables them to give voice to themselves as the subject of their own writing.

Writing the Personal Statement

Often, students' first exposure to the process of generating subject-centered narratives for a specific audience comes when they encounter the task of writing a personal or autobiographical statement for college. McGinty (2002) spent 2 decades teaching English in New Jersey public high schools and worked as an associate director of admissions at Sarah Lawrence College. She conducted a study about high school students' experiences writing the college admissions essay and found that, for many students, "A frequent reaction was 'I've never done anything like this before!' . . . [These students] had rarely written personal narratives, and they had never been judged on their ability to do so."

For most high school seniors, few tasks in the college application process loom as large as the task of writing the personal statement. The personal statement is where students are asked to place themselves at the center of their writing. Whereas the focus of the secondary English classroom is generally on exploring the literature and ideas of others, in the college English classroom and in humanities-based disciplines in general, the focus often expands to include the exploration of one's self through subjects. The personal statement is where students may first begin to tackle this genre of personal and autobiographical writing.

According to McGinty (2012), when writing a personal statement for college, "The essay should be you, in your own words. . . . [L]ike the moment in the Wizard of Oz when the screen goes from black and white to color, the essay can light up and personalize your self-presentation. . . . It is an opportunity to show the admission committee a little about yourself, your insights, your enthusiasm, and your writing ability" (p. 14). Unfortunately, many students receive little guidance in how to write in this genre. School counselors often do not have the time to devote to working with students on individual components of their applications and may not be trained to do so. For many students, especially first-generation college students and students from other traditionally underserved backgrounds, family members and friends may be unable to give specific assistance (McGinty, 2001).

To help them make the transition to college, many students turn to their high school English teachers. In addition to helping prepare students for the rigors of college-level reading, writing, and critical thinking, these educators tend to be called upon to write recommendation letters for students, guide and edit their personal statements, coach them in interviewing skills, and even help them apply for financial aid. In Dickter and Charity Hudley's (2013) survey of college students, around 20% of them stated that teachers in general had been the most important people guiding them through the college application process, and many of these students named their English teacher as the person who wrote their recommendation letters and helped them write their personal statements. Eighty percent of students, however, received no in-school support, reporting either that their help came from family, friends, and nonschool-based mentors, or from no one.

The goal of preparing students to write a personal statement—that is, to create compelling subject-centered narrative prose—is therefore particularly relevant to secondary English educators as their students seek to transition to postsecondary environments. But learning how to write a good personal essay can be challenging, and it is not a genre that is easy to teach. It may sound to students as though the personal statement requires them to consider universal issues or to claim that they are driven to "do something big." As a result, as many educators can attest, students often write in ways that make broad but generic claims about their uniqueness or that refer in general terms to their life circumstances, without providing specifics. To admissions staff, however, vague personal statements can read as unremarkable and bland, and essays that make grandiose claims can read as empty. The question of how to make the personal statement *personal* is a question of how to effectively insert the student as subject with authentic voice into the work, in order to distinguish the essay from the rest of the stack.

When sitting down to write a personal statement, many students claim that they "have nothing to say," that they are "too boring," and that "nothing ever happens to me that's worth writing about." They may feel stuck by not knowing what personal material is appropriate to include, or they may struggle to discuss just one or two events out of the many that seem meaningful. Recall the linguistic and literary autobiography exercise we shared in Box 1.1 on p. 6 as a means for exploring the role of language, culture, and identity in our own lives. This tool can provide an introspective lens to help students identify specific biographical, cultural, literary, and linguistic elements that might otherwise go unnoticed and to select significant personal anecdotes to anchor their narratives. Is the student a first-, second-, or third-generation American? The first family member to graduate from high school or to go to college? Or is college a longstanding tradition? Are languages other than English spoken at home? Has the student had a significant travel or migratory experience that led to cross-cultural insight? Has the student ever been prevented from finishing or perfecting something because of an external circumstance? For students from underserved groups in particular, there may be a wellspring of powerful experiences to draw upon in writing their personal statements, which they may rarely have been encouraged to express in writing or may not have known would be valued. Now is an opportunity for these students to shine.

The goal of developing their voices and placing themselves at the center of a well-crafted oral or written narrative is relevant throughout students' academic journeys. Our linguistic and literary autobiography exercise can be adapted for students from elementary school onward, to help them gain facility with genres of writing that incorporate attention to biography. We ask our own students in college and graduate school to write linguistic and literary autobiographies, and Perryman-Clark (2013) developed a literacy autobiography assignment to use with first-year college students. These types of autobiographies align with the framework of biography-driven culturally responsive teaching, in which educators instruct culturally and linguistically diverse students in ways that draw on their unique backgrounds, incorporate their perspectives, and build on their strengths (Herrera, 2010; Zentella, 2005).

One of the middle school educators who worked with us used an exercise that many educators may be familiar with: the "I Am From" poem, based on the poem "Where I'm From," written by Kentucky-born writer and educator George Ella Lyon (1999). In this exercise, used at the beginning of the school year, the educator asked each student to write a poem that followed the format of Lyon's poem. She explained: "The 'I Am From' poem is my favorite way to learn about who my students are because it invites them to think about the tastes, sayings, people, and environments they know and love best—their own." The educator described how she enjoys "giving my students the time and space to share their ideas as they trickle to the surface, then letting them settle into silence to play with word choice, rhythm, and line breaks. When they are ready for an audience, sharing the final product with each other is an important step to building community within the group." The "I Am From" poem can therefore tap into specific aspects of students' lives that they might have taken for granted or that they might not have realized were different from their classmates' experiences. Other educators have explored variations on this theme, adapting it for students in later grades. In Box 5.6, a high school English educator explained how she uses a Personal Family History project to engage her 10th-graders in exploring their family's language, culture, and history.

BOX 5.6. AN EDUCATOR'S VIGNETTE: The Personal Family History Project

Julie Hildbold,
10th-Grade Honors English Teacher,
AP English Language and Composition Teacher, and Debate Coach

I operate on the principle that students, regardless of their first language or level of language, are the future leaders of the nation. We need to empower them with language, self-respect, and skills. We need to value their language of origin. I was raised in the United States but my father was Greek. His parents never really mastered English, but he and his brothers and sisters had to read the newspaper from cover-to-cover to their father each day. In their small town there was no ESL assistance or special program for them to ease into English, but their parents insisted they learn. All of my father's siblings went to college and had fascinating careers: pilot, superintendent, teacher, government leader.

In my classroom, the Personal Family History is a project that is developed by each student over an entire semester, beginning in September and culminating in a student booklet. Interviewing, drafting, editing, and final production of the student booklet was a very in-depth task, and each student worked very hard on their personal family history projects. Students for whom English is a second language are able to write in their language and translate to English. Students who grew up speaking English can write part of their booklets in the foreign language they are learning in high school, which gives them a sense of the difficulty their English-learning peers may experience. Each student booklet contained:

- Family sayings, inside jokes, etc.
- Special family events and annual celebrations
- A family recipe
- A profile of an admired or interesting relative
- A family history or story of family origin
- Maps and a family tree
- A letter to a family member

At the end of the semester, each student's project was displayed, and students prepared their family recipe for the class. The feast was a culmination and celebration of food of different cultures. We lined the hallway with long tables and enjoyed an incredible buffet of food made by our students and families. The Personal Family History project was a success and was acknowledged in our county's newspaper. It became so popular that other classes joined in the next year, and it became an annual project.

The linguistic and literary autobiography, the "I Am From" poem, and the Personal Family History project are excellent examples of exercises that help all students, not just literature-minded students or college-prep students, write and speak about themselves in ways that are true to their experiences and that incorporate their authentic voices. These assignments can also build upon each other to become the milestone narratives that students will need once they leave the secondary English classroom. What begins in the middle grades as an "I Am From" poem can be turned into a short essay in the early high school years, much like the biographical homework assignment that Langston Hughes recalled writing in his poem, "Theme for English B," which we referenced in Chapter 4 (Box 4.7, pp. 92–93).

The instructor said:
  Go home and write
  a page tonight.
  And let that page come out of you—
  Then, it will be true.
I wonder if it's that simple?

In high school, students can develop these writing assignments into linguistic and literary autobiographies, which can then be directly adapted into personal statements for college applications, essays for scholarship competitions, and even cover letters for a job. As Hughes implies, while it certainly is not "simple," the task of writing a personal statement can be facilitated when students build upon subject-centered prose that they have developed over the years.

Incorporating Authentic Language

In subject-centered writing, students must carefully strike a balance between expressing themselves in a narrative style that is moving and personal and one that other readers (such as admissions officers or professors) will understand. In addition to the personality of the writer, the quality of the prose is a primary basis on which students' writing is judged. To produce high-quality autobiographical writing therefore requires the successful marriage of authentic voice with facility in standardized English. Students must not write so idiosyncratically that they hinder their chances of being understood, but at the same time they must not be so bound to the formulas of standardized English that they strip away their identity. In this section, we explore how secondary English educators can guide students to produce subject-centered narratives that incorporate their personal voices, flow from their own experiences, and capture the attention and imagination of readers, while also being comprehensible to a target audience (Ball & Lardner, 2005).

To begin, it is worth pausing to consider the somewhat ironic point that high school students who have often been trained to take the "I" out of their writing and not "write like they talk" are now being challenged to reinsert their personality and voice at the pinnacle of their high school careers when they write for a personal statement for college admission. It may feel unfamiliar or unsettling for students to be asked to incorporate subjective elements that they previously may have been trained not to use, particularly when they are also hearing the message that the personal essay is a serious piece of writing that can determine their acceptance to college and therefore their futures. It can be surprising for many students, and even some educators, to hear that it is not only acceptable but even encouraged to incorporate subjectivity, particularly in the form of personal anecdotes and authentic language, into the college admissions essay. Rather than favoring the strict use of standardized English in students' personal statements, admissions staff value when students incorporate their voices, which can include the use of language variation. These insights can especially empower students who have stories to tell in diverse voices.

Of course, no matter how powerful the story, students' essays that are wholly "written like they talk" are rarely going to find a receptive audience among admissions counselors or college professors. In general, student essays are considered most readable when they follow basic essay conventions. The use of introductions, thesis sentences, transition words, and concluding language can eliminate a tremendous amount of confusion in an otherwise well thought out idea, as can following general conventions of spelling and punctuation. So where does the linguistic flavor come in? "How much" and "what kind" of linguistic uniqueness should students incorporate into personal essays?

One of the ways for students to incorporate their unique voice is through quoted dialogue that maintains original linguistic elements such as syntax, tone, vocabulary, metaphors, and idioms. In Box 5.7, Clare Trow, guidance counselor at an independent high school, wrote a vignette about how to successfully incorporate voice into a personal statement. As we read in Clare's essay, she surveyed admissions counselors for their reactions to a sample student essay that included the line, "This ain't no joke! You best not move!" This line contains language variation, including *ain't* and *You best not*, both common in Southern and African American varieties of English. Many of the admissions counselors found this use of language variation compelling, as it gives a sense of the tone of the interaction and of the speakers involved. Clare originally wrote this essay in one of our workshops in 2009. Seeking to reach a wider audience, she then published a version of it in *NextStepU*, a magazine to help high school students plan for college (Trow, 2010).

BOX 5.7. AN EDUCATOR'S VIGNETTE: Creating Your Signature Style: Putting Your Voice into Your College Essay

Clare Trow, College Counselor

"you shall above all things be glad and young
For if you're young, whatever life you wear

it will become you; and if you are glad
whatever's living will yourself become."

Quick, identify the errors in the sentence above.

Sorry, that was a trick question. The stanza is from the poem "you shall above all things be glad and young," by the great poet, E. E. Cummings. Everyone knows he's a genius who went to Harvard, and geniuses never make errors in their writing, especially errors like using lowercase or uppercase letters where there should be the opposite and misusing punctuation. Right?

Wrong. E. E. Cummings became famous and respected precisely because of his errors; he made them all the time. The difference between his errors and your mistakes that bring your grade down for each red mark in the margin on an English paper is that his work had a system that became known as his signature style.

In the poem "anyone lived in a pretty how town," Cummings uses a pattern of errors; he puts the wrong type of object with the wrong type of verb—as in, "slept their dream." He didn't get a bunch of red marks, though. He manages to convey greater meaning and a stronger sense of action by putting these words together in a way that you don't normally see.

But you're facing the task of writing a stack of college essays and have no idea why I'm going on about this poet. I'm bringing up E. E. Cummings because I want to make a point to you: Think a little bit out of the box when you sit down to write your college essay. Cummings had a signature style that worked for him. Create one out of your own everyday voice that works for you. As a result, you will gain some attention by submitting something the admissions counselors don't normally see.

I recently surveyed close to 60 admissions counselors from colleges and universities across the United States, small to large in size, public and private, with top academic programs ranging from business to engineering to (yes) English and communications. I found out some interesting things.

First of all, 100% of them rated strong writing skills as at least an "important" contributor to academic success, and 54% said writing skills were "critical" to success. Your essay is your first chance to convince them that you've got the tools and the talent to get the job done on their campus.

No surprise that 93% of the admissions counselors surveyed will rank your transcript as the most important factor in your application review. The second highest ranked factor is your SAT or ACT test score. What should be waiting patiently next in line? The Essay. And your essay is something over which you can have complete control in the next few months.

In my office this fall, Jeff Williams, the Assistant Director of Admissions for Boston University, where they received over 37,000 applications last year alone, said it best when he was speaking with my students: "Your essay is your interview."

So what are they hoping to learn about you? In my survey over 80% of the admissions counselors rated learning about your "character" and "personality" as their top priorities when reading an essay. Only 8% most want to hear about your accomplishments—leave the list of activities to the application; focus on what makes you tick. And the number one hallmark of a strong essay, "honest and genuine" came in at almost 90%. Other top-ranked elements include "clarity of message" (84%), "strong grammar" and "organized writing" (71% each).

Okay, fine, but where do I start, you ask. Let's go back to E. E. Cummings. He relied on patterns in his poems that can become more familiar to a reader. These patterns became his signature style, his voice. You have a voice, too. And here's the best part: You don't have to work to create it; it's already a part of who you are. All of us use predictable and reliable speech patterns with our language depending on who we are, where we're from, and probably most importantly who we're talking to—is it your grandmother, your best friend, or your English teacher? (See, I did it just there: I said *who* when I should have said *whom*. But hey, who talks like that anyway?)

When I surveyed the admissions counselors from nearly 60 colleges and universities across the United States, I also included a few sample personal essays written by students and asked the counselors to respond to them. One of the essays I asked my survey respondents to react to had this line in it: "This ain't no joke! You best not move!" I know you can spot the grammar mistakes there, but listen to this: 39% of the counselors surveyed said that this essay would not only *not* have a negative impact on admissions review but would actually help the student get in if she ended up on the cusp of the accepted applicants. Why? I think it is because the essay from that student included her own voice as well as strong writing in "standardized English"—the kind of English your teachers are working with you to perfect (that whole *who* vs. *whom* thing, for example). And unlike E. E. Cummings, whose poetry can sometimes be confusing, this student didn't leave the admissions counselors struggling through literary analysis to get to her meaning—trust me, they won't take the time. The student provided enough of a structure surrounding her voice to help the admissions counselors along. The admissions counselors specifically commented on how much they liked the "authenticity" of this student's essay and how it felt more "credible" since the readers were able to more easily visualize the story she was telling.

Let me take my audience analogy one step further. You probably talk one way to your English teacher and another way to your grandmother and another to your best friend. You probably also wear different clothes to church and to school and when you're lounging on the sofa on a Saturday afternoon. In your college essay, try to think about talking to your grandma and wearing a comfortable pair of good jeans. You don't want to write your college essay as though you're wearing sweatpants, but at the same time, don't be so uptight that you can hardly breathe in that prom dress, okay?

The lesson for you is: Be true to your voice, while also making sure that your message is clear and that you exhibit good grammar and strong writing along the way. Believe in yourself!

Writing a specific subject-centered narrative that uses authentic language can be much more difficult than writing in grandiose generics, and students often need guidance in how to develop this skill. Recall the authors we discussed in Chapter 4, who incorporate language variation into great works of literature, and the exercises that we provided to prompt students to consider language variation in literature and model their own writing after these authors. Secondary English educators can design real-world–based, authentic assignments that build on students' linguistic skill and that weave college preparation into the curriculum. For instance, high school English educators can give the assignment of writing a personal statement, which prepares students for the college application process. First-generation college-bound students may particularly benefit from individual attention (e.g., direct feedback and student-teacher writing conferences) as they craft their personal essays. In Box 5.8, a high school writing tutor explained how he helps first-generation college-bound students to focus on events, transcribe remembered speech, and create verbal landscapes as they write subject-centered personal essays that incorporate authentic dialogue. By practicing these skills, students can learn to translate their own voice and the voices of people in their communities onto the page.

BOX 5.8. AN EDUCATOR'S VIGNETTE: Helping First-Generation College-Bound Students Write Personal Statements and Essays

Blake Williams,
High School Writing Tutor

I work as a high school writing tutor at a community center in Baltimore, Maryland. Many of the students who attend the after-school program there are the first in their families to graduate from high school, and most are the first in their families to go to college.

For several years, I have helped students write their personal statements and essays. I help them navigate the college admissions process, which is often overwhelming for students who are trying to figure it out on their own. Many of them are trying to write a personal statement at the same time that they are filling out a vast number of forms, trying to keep dates in their heads, and collecting information for financial aid. Writing and rewriting an essay feels to them like something they don't have much time or patience for, so when I work with them I try to break the big project of writing a personal statement down into separate, more manageable tasks that build toward a coherent and powerful essay.

Students are often asked to respond to one of several prompts when writing college essays. Left to their own devices, students often get distracted by the question of which prompt is best to choose, get discouraged by what can seem like difficult or confusing wording, or latch onto a word or phrase in the prompt and go off topic, writing in ways that address the question too narrowly. I find it more valuable to help students first figure out which powerful stories they can authentically tell and then tailor them to fit a prompt. This is never difficult to do, because many prompts are either open-ended or seek to plumb students' personal experiences.

I begin by having the student make a list of specific, concrete events that were complex or complicated, that were hard to face or difficult to deal with, that were emotional, or that were weighty in some way. I then ask the student to convince me, verbally, which one of these events was the most powerful or transformative. This process helps the student narrow down the list of appropriate and compelling life experiences. Also, by talking out why one topic is better than another, the student can figure out what works before spending time writing it out.

Sometimes, I find that students from traditionally underserved backgrounds will seek to take the personal element out of their personal statements. Some students say that they feel uncomfortable talking about personal difficulties in their essays. Some worry that they are exploiting these events for college, and, more frequently, they sometimes think that admissions staff won't want to hear what they have been through. Others fear that they are simply complaining or telling family secrets. Some of them, in wanting to make themselves sound college-worthy, feel that addressing things like poverty can make them sound too weak to be successful.

I firmly believe that students should never have to write about any events that they are uncomfortable writing about. At the same time, students often don't realize that their own lives, their truthful experiences, are what can be told most powerfully in a personal essay. They may not fully understand that there can be value in telling how they have overcome difficulty or even tragedy and that these challenges, when effectively framed, can be seen by readers as evidence of their strength and determination. It requires a level of trust for students to tell me about things they have overcome, but once they decide what to tell me, we work together to help them decide what they feel comfortable sharing with outside readers. By the end of the process, students feel proud and eager to share how they have overcome obstacles in their lives.

Once the student and I have figured out which one or two events are the most compelling to share in a personal essay, I have the student try to tell the story using authentic language, with no framing or editing at this point. Even if the student's story sounds like stream of consciousness, it can be shaped and refined later. I ask the student to try to draw me a verbal picture of a scene from memory, which will later lend descriptive detail to the essay. I also guide the student to remember dialogue, often by asking questions, such as, "What did you say next? What did they say back to you?" We try to build a transcript of things that might have been said, even if the student doesn't end up using it all in the final version. I encourage the student to transcribe that dialogue to the written page in a way that captures accurately the sounds and tone of what is being said, and I leave those transcripts of dialogue completely to the student's discretion.

After the student has created powerful, rich descriptions that include authentic dialogue, we talk about framing—that is, how this event relates to the student's goal of attending college. I ask questions such as, how did this event help you or hinder you in school? How do you feel now that you have overcome this personal challenge? How did this event shape people around you—for instance, by inspiring siblings, by altering relationships with guardians, or by bringing family or friends closer together, or by driving people apart? Do you think you will be a stronger person and college student because of what you have gone through, and why? How do your personal experiences relate to what you think you might want to major in in college or what career you plan to have?

After the student has a sense of what framing to use, and after the student has thought about specific scenes and described them in rich detail, only then do I have the student write the essay, drawing examples, dialogue, and language from the notes we have developed. I encourage students to think of this point forward as the actual drafting of the essay, rather than simply cutting and pasting from notes they have typed. (It helps if the notes and dialogue have been handwritten up to this point, so that students must make deliberate linguistic and stylistic choices as they craft their first draft.) The final step is to ask the student to reread their writing with an eye for mechanics and see what might need to be revised.

I have found that this technique is an excellent way to help students (especially those from traditionally underrepresented backgrounds) realize the strengths that they have and connect these strengths to their determination to succeed academically. I can say, firsthand, that these strategies have worked. Students I have tutored have gone on to college—small liberal arts colleges, larger universities, historically Black colleges and universities, local schools, out-of-state schools—and they all started by writing a personal essay.

We have used the task of writing a personal statement for college as a touchstone for our discussion of subject-centered writing because it is so salient to secondary English students and educators. But the lessons that can be learned from analyzing how to craft a powerful, authentic personal essay are not limited to college admission. They can also be used to reach students who are less invested in the secondary English curriculum. DeBord (2003) discussed how she inspired a group of otherwise disengaged 10th-grade English students from rural communities in southwest Virginia to draw on personal experience to create narratives and then participate with other students in a class performance. She asked, "What if someone had been soliciting young people's personal stories since kindergarten? Would they now be alienated and eager to drop out of school?" (p. 366). For secondary English educators who are tasked with teaching a range of students how to do many things at once—how to communicate, in different modes and genres, for different purposes, and how to read and critically analyze the texts that others have written, it can help to consider these goals as interconnected, rather than separate. As one educator who worked with us put it, "I have realized that literacy instruction needs to be inclusive. I can't teach just subject-verb agreement on its own and then do personal writing and then British Literature. I have to integrate all of it for students to truly learn and extend their knowledge." Personal writing is not a just a creative add-on but rather a tool that can be incorporated whether instruction is centered on literacy or literature.

For college-bound students, knowing how to write subject-centered and biography-driven narratives is more than just a skill they need for their personal essays in order to get to college; it is also a skill they will use in college. Identity, culture, and social interaction become more central as topics of study in postsecondary environments, and in many college classrooms and in graduate school, subject-centered writing is highly valued. In Box 5.9, sociolinguist and professor Dr. Elaine Richardson discusses how writing that incorporated biographical elements was a key element of her doctoral dissertation. Ultimately, her research and writing evolved into several books in which she speaks to people from her home communities, drawing upon these discourse styles and connecting them to academic writing and exploration.

BOX 5.9. A SOCIOLINGUIST'S VIGNETTE: Writing for the Hood Girl in Me: PGD (Po' Girl on Dope) to PhD and Other Language Dilemmas

Dr. Elaine Richardson,
Professor of Literacy Studies and Education at the Ohio State University

My subject is myself and my unfolding understanding of discourse and society, the bodies of knowledge, ideologies, and social literacies that mediate my experiences of the world; it is how I became who I am.

I graduated with my PhD from Michigan State University in 1996. In my dissertation, I addressed a problem that still exists: How do we make ourselves the subject of the writing classroom and indeed all classrooms, so that we don't have to become alienated from ourselves in order to learn a subject? How do we embrace the language and literacies of students in order to teach about the intricate relations of language and society?

My educational experiences, for the most part, taught me that I was illiterate, that my language was ignorant, and that I needed to get rid of my culture in order to be successful in the academy and the mainstream. There was a disconnect between what teachers knew about my home language and how this language was essential to my culture, my history, my identity, my literacy.

My dissertation project sought to develop a curriculum that would contribute to filling this void. I learned sophisticated theories of linguistics, histories and cultural studies of Black languages, their oral and literate traditions. I developed my research design, administered it to Black students, saw promising results, wrote my dissertation, and eventually, expanded these studies and turned my dissertation into my first book, *African American Literacies* (Richardson, 2003b). I've written subsequent scholarly books that in some way seek to add to the understanding of literacy, education, and culture.

What did those books do for people from my hood? Many of them will never open those books. Many of them will never come through these doors. I need to reach people to invite them in, validate their lives.

When activist educators from historically oppressed groups tell their stories of rising from poverty to PhD, or General Education Degree (GED) to PhD, or from whatever less than mainstream "at-risk" for failure position to "American success story," they do so hoping that, in narrating, the exception can become the rule. Shout to Sojourner Truth who said, "I don't read such small stuff as letters, I read men and nations."

It's taken me 17 years to get to where I am today, to write for me, my people, using my own language.

CONCLUSION

Throughout the secondary English curriculum, educators can inspire in students a lifelong passion for stories well told—those of others as well as their own. Great literature would not exist without compelling narratives and the authors who tell them, and our students also have their own compelling narratives to tell. When students are empowered to engage with and build upon their own language and the voices of their homes and communities, they develop their linguistic agency, which becomes a resource for them to draw upon as they transition beyond high school. They also develop the linguistic awareness to view the language differences of others not as deficits but as assets, as threads in the woven fabric of our multicultural society. By cultivating all students' understanding of and respect for language variation, secondary English educators are well positioned to help students learn the valuable skill of being able to communicate with diverse audiences in their everyday lives.

Our messages of voice, identity, communication, and empowerment that we have shared in this book are not just relevant for students; they are also relevant for us as educators. Like their students, secondary English educators are engaged in "doing language" every day, operating as linguistic agents in homes and communities and as instructors and mentors in classrooms and schools. Educators who have developed knowledge about and critical awareness of language, language variation, culture, and communication can directly apply this information to the mission of helping all students achieve. As more partnerships between secondary and postsecondary educators are established, channels of communication are broadened, and important pedagogical insights are shared. By understanding how language is central to the lives of our students and to our own lives, we bring ourselves into the conversation about how to honor and cultivate diversity of expression as we educate the next generation of readers and writers, speakers and scholars, dreamers and thinkers.

References

Ahern, L. M. (2001). Language and agency. *Annual Review of Anthropology, 30*(1), 109–137.

Alim, H. S., & Smitherman, G. (2012). *Articulate while Black: Barack Obama, language, and race in the U.S.* New York: Oxford University Press.

Anderson, E. (2000). *Code of the street.* New York: Norton.

Anderson, W., & Groff, P. (1972). *A new look at children's literature.* Belmont, CA: Wadsworth Publishing Co.

Appleman, D. (2009). *Critical encounters in high school English: Teaching literary theory to adolescents* (2nd ed.). New York: Teachers College Press.

Arai, M., & Thoursie, P. S. (2009). Renouncing personal names: An empirical examination of surname change and earnings. *Journal of Labor Economics, 27*(1), 127–147.

Asim, J. (2007). *The n word: Who can say it, who shouldn't, and why.* New York: Houghton Mifflin Harcourt.

Baker, D. S. (2011). N-word or no n-word? That is the question. *Teaching Tolerance.* Retrieved from www.tolerance.org/blog/n-word-or-no-n-word-question

Balester, V. (1993). *Cultural divide: A study of African-American college-level writers.* Portsmouth, NH: Boynton/Cook.

Ball, A. F., & Lardner, T. (2005). *African American literacies unleashed: Vernacular English and the composition classroom.* Carbondale: Southern Illinois University Press.

Banks, A. J. (2011). *Digital griots: African American rhetoric in a multimedia age.* Carbondale: National Council of Teachers of English/Conference on College Composition and Communication and Southern Illinois University Press.

Banks, J., & Banks, C. (Eds.). (2007). *Multicultural education: Issues and perspectives* (7th ed.). New York: John Wiley & Sons.

Baron, D. (2012). *A better pencil: Readers, writers, and the digital revolution.* New York: Oxford University Press.

Baugh, J. (1999). *Out of the mouths of slaves: African American language and educational malpractice.* Austin: University of Texas Press.

Behrens, S. (2012). Why every professor needs Linguistics 101. *The Chronicle of Higher Education.* Retrieved from www.chronicle.com/article/Why-Every-Professor-Needs/130855/

Bernstein, C. G. (Ed.). (1994). *The text and beyond: Essays in literary linguistics.* Tuscaloosa: University of Alabama Press.

Bertrand, M., & Mullainathan, S. (2004). Are Emily and Greg more employable than Lakisha and Jamal? A field experiment on labor market discrimination. *American Economic Review, 94*(4), 991–1013.

Biber, D., & Finegan, E. (1994). *Sociolinguistic perspectives on register*. New York: Oxford University Press.

Black, R. W. (2009). English-language learners, fan communities, and 21st century skills. *Journal of Adolescent and Adult Literacy, 52*(8), 688–697.

Blank, P. (1996). *Broken English: Dialects and the politics of language in Renaissance writings*. New York: Routledge.

Bonfiglio, T. P. (2002). *Race and the rise of standard American*. Berlin: Mouton de Gruyter.

Bourdieu, P. (1991). *Language and symbolic power*. New York: Harvard University Press.

Brandon, K. (2009). Investing in education: The American Graduation Initiative. Retrieved from www.whitehouse.gov/blog/Investing-in-Education-The-American-Graduation-Initiative

Burch, A. (2012). Facebook page challenges how Blacks define themselves. *Miami Herald*. Retrieved from www.nairaland.com/871368/african-americans-now-want-called-blacks/3

Calarco, J. M. (2011). "I need help!" Social class and children's help-seeking in elementary school. *American Sociological Review, 76*(6), 862–882.

Carr, R. L. (1974). A study of the attitudes of sixth grade children toward literary characters represented as speaking nonstandard dialects of American English (doctoral dissertation). University of Illinois at Urbana-Champaign.

Carter, P. L. (2007). *Keepin' it real: School success beyond Black and White*. New York: Oxford University Press.

Charity Hudley, A. H., Harris, J., Hayes, J., Ikeler, K., & Squires, A. (2008). Service-learning as an introduction to sociolinguistics and linguistic equality. *American Speech, 83*(2), 237–251.

Charity Hudley, A. H. (2012). Teaching about English language variations. In J. A. Banks (Ed.), *The encyclopedia of diversity in education* (pp. 796–799). Washington, DC: Sage Publications.

Charity Hudley, A. H. (2013a). Linguistics and social activism. In R. Cameron, C. Lucas, & R. Bayley (Eds.), *The Oxford handbook of sociolinguistics* (pp. 812–831). New York: Oxford University Press.

Charity Hudley, A. H. (2013b). Sociolinguistic engagement in schools: Collecting and sharing data. In C. Mallinson, B. Childs, & G. Van Herk (Eds.), *Data collection in sociolinguistics: Methods and applications* (pp. 269–280). New York: Routledge.

Charity Hudley, A. H., & Mallinson, C. (2011). *Understanding English language variation in U.S. schools*. New York: Teachers College Press.

Chen-Hayes, S. F., Chen, M., & Athar, N. (1999). Challenging linguicism: Action strategies for counselors and client-colleagues. In J. Lewis & L. Bradley (Eds.), *Advocacy in counseling: Counselors, clients, & community* (pp. 21–31). Greensboro, NC: ERIC Counseling and Student Services Clearinghouse.

Childs, B., & Mallinson, C. (2006). The significance of lexical items in the construction of ethnolinguistic identity: A case study of adolescent spoken and online language. *American Speech*, *81*(1), 3–30.

Christenbury, L. (1996). Race differences: A White teacher and a native son. In B. M. Power & R. S. Hubbard (Eds.), *Oops: What we learn when our teaching fails* (pp. 77–81). York, ME: Stenhouse Publishers.

Christianson, D. (2002). *Language use in multiethnic literature for young adults*. ERIC Research report. Retrieved from www.eric.ed.gov/ERICWebPortal/search/detailmini.jsp?_nfpb=true&_&ERICExtSearch_SearchValue_0=ED477555&ERICExtSearch_SearchType_0=no&accno=ED477555

Clayton, T. (2013). The Oscars, Quvenzhané, and the c-word. *Uptown Magazine*. Retrieved from www.uptownmagazine.com/2013/02/the-oscars-quvenzhane-the-c-word/

College Board (2010). English language. Retrieved from www.collegeboard.com/student/testing/ap/sub_englang.html

Common Core State Standards Initiative. (2012a). *English Language Arts standards: College and career readiness anchor standards for language*. Retrieved from http://www.corestandards.org/ELA-Literacy/CCRA/L

Common Core State Standards Initiative. (2012b). *Key points in English Language Arts*. Retrieved from www.corestandards.org/about-the-standards/key-points-in-english-language-arts

Common Core State Standards Initiative. (2012c). *Students who are college and career ready in reading, writing, speaking, listening, and language*. Retrieved from www.corestandards.org/ELA-Literacy/introduction/students-who-are-college-and-career-ready-in-reading-writing-speaking-listening-language

Craig, H. K., & Washington, J. A. (2006). *Malik goes to school: Examining the language skills of African American students from preschool to fifth grade*. Mahwah, NJ: Lawrence Erlbaum.

Craven, C. (2011). Exploring the power of the n-word. *Teaching Tolerance*. Retrieved from www.tolerance.org/blog/exploring-power-n-word

Crystal, D. (2003). *The encyclopedia of the English language*. New York: Cambridge University Press.

Crystal, D. (2008). 2b or not 2b? *The Guardian*. Retrieved from www.guardian.co.uk/books/2008/jul/05/saturdayreviewsfeatres.guardianreview

Crystal, D. (2012). *English as a global language*. New York: Cambridge University Press.

Curzan, A. (2000). English historical corpora in the classroom: The intersection of teaching and research. *Journal of English Linguistics*, *28*(1), 77–89.

DeBord, A. (2003). Telling your own story: A story illumination project. *Journal of Appalachian Studies*, 9(2), 363–376.

Delpit, L. D., & Dowdy, J. K. (Eds.). (2008). *The skin that we speak: Thoughts on language and culture in the classroom*. New York: New Press.

DeRosier, L. S. (1999). *Creeker: A woman's journey*. Lexington: University Press of Kentucky.

DeYoung, A. J. (1995). Constructing and staffing the cultural bridge: The school as change agent in rural Appalachia. *Anthropology & Education Quarterly*, *26*(2), 168–192.

Dickter, C. L., & Charity Hudley, A. H. (2013). Using the pre-college and college experiences of underrepresented students to address inequalities in undergraduate research opportunities. Manuscript in preparation.

Dickter, C. L., & Newton, V. A. (2013). To confront or not to confront: Non-targets' evaluations of and responses to racist comments. *Journal of Applied Social Psychology*, *43*: E262–E275.

Douglass, T. (2006). Denise Giardina: Resurrecting the dead, recognizing the human: Interview by Thomas Douglass (1998). In J. Lang (Ed.), *Appalachia and beyond: Conversations with writers from the Mountain South* (pp. 241–258). Knoxville: University of Tennessee Press.

Du Bois, W. E. B. (1903). *The souls of Black folk*. Chicago: A.C. McClurg & Co., University Press John Wilson and Son.

Dufresne, J. (2003). *The lie that tells a truth: A guide to writing fiction*. New York: Norton.

Dunn, P. A., & Lindblom, K. (2003). Why revitalize grammar? *The English Journal*, 92(3), 43–50.

Dunstan, S. B. (2013). The influence of speaking a dialect of Appalachian English on the college experience (doctoral dissertation). North Carolina State University.

Eckert, P. (1989). *Jocks and burnouts: Social categories and identity in the high school*. New York: Teachers College Press.

Eckert, P., & McConnell-Ginet, S. (2003). *Language and gender*. New York: Cambridge University Press.

Erickson, F. (2007). Culture in society and in educational practices. In J. Banks & C. Banks (Eds.), *Multicultural education: Issues and perspectives*. (7th ed., pp. 33–58). New York: John Wiley & Sons.

Ferris, W. R. (2011, July). Keynote address. The Clarksville Writers' Conference, Clarksville, TN.

Fisher, D., & Frey, N. (2011). Academic language in the secondary classroom. *Principal Leadership, 11*(6), 64–66.

Fitzgerald, S. (1979). *The habit of being: Letters of Flannery O'Connor*. New York: Farrar, Straus and Giroux.

Foster, M. (1989). "It's cookin' now": A performance analysis of the speech events of a Black teacher in an urban community college. *Language in Society*, *18*(1), 1–29.

Frazier, I. (2012). Word. *The New Yorker*. Retrieved from www.newyorker.com/talk/2012/03/05/120305ta_talk_frazier

Freese, J. H. (Trans.). (1924). *Aristotle, The art of rhetoric*. Cambridge, MA: Loeb Classical Library/Harvard University Press.

Gay, G. (1994). *A synthesis of scholarship in multicultural education* [Urban Education Monograph Series]. Seattle: NCREL Urban Education Program.

Gee, J. P. (1996). *Social linguistics and literacies: Ideology in discourses* (2nd ed.). New York: Taylor & Francis.

Gibbons, L. (2009). To kill a mockingbird *in the classroom: Walking in someone else's shoes*. Urbana, IL: National Council of Teachers of English.

Gilyard, K. (2011). *True to the language game: African American discourse, cultural politics, and pedagogy*. New York: Routledge.

Giovanni, N. (2002). *Quilting the black eyed pea.* New York: William Morrow.

Goodman, Y. M. (2003). *Valuing language study: Inquiry into language for elementary and middle schools.* Urbana, IL: National Council of Teachers of English.

Grammar Girl. (2011). Should you point out errors? [Podcast]. *Quick and dirty tips for better writing.* Retrieved from www.grammar.quickanddirtytips.com/should-you-point-out-errors

Greenhow, C., & Robelia, E. (2009). Old communication, new literacies: Social network sites as social learning resources. *Journal of Computer-Mediated Communication, 14*(4), 1130–1161.

Hamilton, S. J. (1995). *My name's not Susie: A life transformed by literacy.* Portsmouth, NH: Boynton/Cook.

Hartigan, J., Jr. (2003). Who are these White people?: "Rednecks," "hillbillies," and "white trash" as marked racial subjects. In A. W. Doane & E. Bonilla-Silva (Eds.), *White out: The continuing significance of racism* (pp. 95–111). New York: Routledge.

Heath, S. B. (1983). *Ways with words: Language, life and work in communities and classrooms.* New York: Cambridge University Press.

Heller, J. R. (2003). Toni Cade Bambara's use of African American Vernacular English in "The lesson." *Style, 37*(3), 279–293.

Henderson, A. (2003). What's in a slur? *American Speech, 78*(1), 52–74.

Herrera, S. (2010). *Biography-driven culturally responsive teaching.* New York: Teachers College Press.

Higgs, R., Manning, A., & Miller, J. W. (1995). *Appalachian inside out: Culture and custom.* Knoxville: University of Tennessee Press.

Holloway, K. F. C. (1987). *The character of the word: The texts of Zora Neale Hurston.* Santa Barbara, CA: Praeger.

hooks, b. (1989). *Talking back: Thinking feminist, thinking Black.* Boston: South End Press.

Howard, T. C. (2010). *Why race and culture matter in schools: Closing the achievement gap in America's classrooms.* New York: Teachers College Press.

Hutchings, M., Carrington, B., Francis, B., Skelton, C., Read, B., & Hall, I. (2008). Nice and kind, smart and funny: What children like and want to emulate in their teachers. *Oxford Review of Education, 34*(2), 135–157.

Hymes, D. H. (1966). Two types of linguistic relativity. In W. Bright (Ed.), *Sociolinguistics* (pp. 114–158). The Hague: Mouton.

Hymes, D. H. (1974). *Foundations in sociolinguistics: An ethnographic approach.* Philadelphia: University of Pennsylvania Press.

James R. Squire Office of Policy Research. (2007). *21st-century literacies: A policy research brief.* Urbana, IL: National Council of Teachers of English.

Johnson, F. (2012). *Say this, NOT that to your professor: 36 talking tips for college success.* Bedford, IN: NorLightsPress.

Junco, R., Heiberger, G., & Loken, E. (2011). The effect of Twitter on college student engagement and grades. *Journal of Computer Assisted Learning, 27*(2), 119–132.

Kendall, T., & Wolfram, W. (2009). Local and external language standards in African American English. *Journal of English Linguistics, 37*, 305–330.

Kennedy, R. (2002). *Nigger: The strange career of a troublesome word*. New York: Pantheon.

Kinloch, V. (2010). "To not be a traitor of Black English": Youth perceptions of language rights in an urban context. *Teachers College Record*, *112*(1), 103–141.

Kirkland, D. (2010). Teaching English in a sea of change: Linguistic pluralism and the new English education. *English Education*, *42*(3), 231–235.

Knecht, K. (n.d.). Facing the "n word." *Teaching Tolerance*. Retrieved from www.tolerance.org/activity/facing-n-word

Kress, G. (2003). *Literacy in the new media age*. New York: Routledge.

Labov, W. (1972a). *Language in the inner city: Studies in the Black English Vernacular*. Philadelphia: University of Pennsylvania Press.

Labov, W. (1972b). *Sociolinguistic patterns*. Philadelphia: University of Pennsylvania Press.

Labov, W. (1987). How I got into linguistics and what I got out of it. Retrieved from www.ling.upenn.edu/~wlabov/Papers/HowIgot.html

Labov, W. (1995). Can reading failure be reversed? A linguistic approach to the question. In V. L. Gadsden & D. A. Wagner (Eds.), *Literacy among African-American youth: Issues in learning, teaching, and schooling* (pp. 39–68). Creskill, NJ: Hampton Press.

Lakoff, R. (1975). *Language and woman's place*. New York: Harper & Row.

Lapp, D., Fisher, D., & Frey, N. (2012). Preparing our students as writers. *Voices from the Middle*, *19*(3), 7–9.

Lawrence, A. (2012). Rich media in the classroom. Retrieved from at.blogs.wm.edu/rich-media-in-the-classroom/

Lave, J., & Wenger, E. (1991). *Situated learning: Legitimate peripheral participation*. Cambridge: Cambridge University Press.

Lenhart, A., Arafeh, S., Smith, A., & McGill, A. R. (2008). Writing, technology and teens. *The Pew Internet & American life project*. Retrieved from www.pewinternet.org/Reports/2008/Writing-Technology-and-Teens.aspx

Lenhart, A., Purcell, K., Smith, A., & Zickuhr, K. (2010). Social media and young adults. *The Pew Internet & American life project*. Retrieved from www.pewinternet.org/Reports/2010/Social-Media-and-Young-Adults.aspx

Lieberson, S., & Mikelson, K. S. (1995). Distinctive African American names: An experimental, historical, and linguistic analysis of innovation. *American Sociological Review*, *60*(6), 928–946.

Lindblom, K. (Ed.). (2011). Beyond grammar: The richness of English language [Special issue]. *English Journal*, *100*(4).

Lippi-Green, R. (2011). *English with an accent: Language, ideology and discrimination in the United States*. New York: Routledge.

Locklear, E. A. (2011). *Negotiating a perilous empowerment: Appalachian women's literacies*. Athens: Ohio University Press.

Lorde, A. (1984). *Sister outsider: Essays and speeches*. Berkeley, CA: The Crossing Press.

Lott, E. (1995). Mr. Clemens and Jim Crow: Twain, race and Blackface. In F. G. Robinson (Ed.), *The Cambridge companion to Mark Twain* (pp. 129–152). Cambridge, UK: Cambridge University Press.

Lunsford, A. A., Ruszkiewicz, J. J., & Walters, K. (2012). *Everything's an argument* (6th ed.). New York: Bedford/St. Martin's.

Lyon, G. E. (1999). *Where I'm from*. Retrieved from www.georgeellalyon.com/where.html

MacNeil, R., & Cran, W. (2005). *Do you speak American?: A companion to the PBS television series*. New York: Nan A. Talese.

Macrone, M. (1990). *Brush up your Shakespeare!* New York: Gramercy Books.

Madrid-Campbell, T., & Hughes, J. (n.d.). Linguicism. *Teaching Tolerance*. Retrieved from www.tolerance.org/activity/linguicism

Magee, R. M. (Ed.). (2000). *Conversations with Flannery O'Connor*. Jackson: University Press of Mississippi.

Magnusson, L. (2004). "Voice potential": Language and symbolic capital in *Othello*. In C. M. S. Alexander (Ed.), *Shakespeare and language* (pp. 213–225). New York: Cambridge University Press.

Mallinson, C. (2011). Language in Baltimore. Retrieved from www.baltimorelanguage.com/

Mallinson, C., & Charity Hudley, A. H. (2010). Communicating about communication: Multidisciplinary approaches to educating educators about language variation. *Language and Linguistics Compass, 4* (Sociolinguistics section), 245–257.

Mallinson, C., & Charity Hudley, A. H. (2011). Collaborative research: Assessing the results of sociolinguistic engagement with K–12 STEM education in Maryland and Virginia public and independent schools [Grants 1050938 and 1051056 to the National Science Foundation, Division of Behavioral and Cognitive Sciences, Developmental & Learning Sciences Program].

Mallinson, C., & Charity Hudley, A. H. (forthcoming). Partnering through science: developing linguistic insight to address educational inequality for culturally and linguistically diverse students in U.S. STEM education. *Language and Linguistics Compass* (Education & Pedagogy section).

Mallinson, C., Charity Hudley, A. H., Strickling, L. R., & Figa, M. (2011). A conceptual framework for promoting linguistic and educational change. *Language and Linguistics Compass, 5* (Education & Pedagogy section), 441–453.

Mallinson, C., Childs, B., & Van Herk, G. (Eds.). (2013). *Data collection in sociolinguistics: Methods and applications*. New York: Routledge.

Mallinson, C., & Kendall, T. (2013). Interdisciplinary approaches. In R. Cameron, C. Lucas, & R. Bayley (Eds.), *The Oxford handbook of sociolinguistics* (pp. 153–171). New York: Oxford University Press.

McGinty, S. M. (2001). Missing persons: Who needs more help with the college application essay? *Harvard Education Letter, 17*(6). Retrieved from www.hepg.org/hel/article/180

McGinty, S. M. (2002). The application essay. *The Chronicle of Higher Education*. Retrieved from www.chronicle.com/article/The-Application-Essay/15324/

McGinty, S. M. (2012). *The college application essay: All-new fifth edition*. New York: The College Board.

McIntosh, P. (1988). White privilege: Unpacking the invisible knapsack. Excerpted from *White privilege and male privilege: A personal account of coming to see correspondences through work in women's studies*. Wellesley, MA: Wellesley College Center for Research on Women.

Meier, T. (2008). *Black communications and learning to read: Building on children's linguistic and cultural strengths*. Mahwah, NJ: Lawrence Erlbaum.

Microaggressions Project (2010–2013). Microaggressions. Retrieved from www.microaggressions.com

Minnick, L. C. (2004). *Dialect and dichotomy: Literary representations of African American speech*. Tuscaloosa: University of Alabama Press.

Minnick, L. C. (2010). Dialect literature and English in the USA: Standardization and national linguistic identity. In R. Hickey (Ed.), *Varieties of English in writing: The written word as linguistic evidence* (pp. 163–195). Amsterdam: John Benjamins.

Moorhead, A. (2011). Carol Ann Duffy: "Poems are a form of texting." *The Guardian*. Retrieved from www.guardian.co.uk/education/2011/sep/05/carol-ann-duffy-poetry-texting-competition

Morgan, M. (2004). "I'm every woman": Black women's (dis)placement in women's language study. In M. Bucholtz (Ed.), *Language and woman's place: Text and commentaries* (pp. 252–259). New York: Oxford University Press.

Morrell, E., Dueñas, R., Garcia, V., & López, J. (2013). *Critical media pedagogy: Teaching for achievement in city schools*. New York: Teachers College Press.

Morrison, T. (1993). Nobel lecture. *The Nobel Foundation*. Retrieved from www.nobelprize.org/nobel_prizes/literature/laureates/1993/morrison-lecture.html

Morrison, T. (1998). This amazing, troubling book. In T. Cooley (Ed.) & M. Twain, *Adventures of Huckleberry Finn* (pp. 385–392). New York: Norton.

National Council of Teachers of English. (2003). Resolution on affirming the CCCC "Students' right to their own language." Retrieved from www.ncte.org/positions/statements/affirmingstudents

National Council of Teachers of English & International Reading Association. (1996). *Standards for the English language arts*. Urbana, IL: National Council of Teachers of English and Newark, DE: International Reading Association.

Nettels, E. (1988). *Language, race, and social class in Howells's America*. Lexington: University Press of Kentucky.

Palmer, N. (2012). Speaking in class is always optional. *Sociology source*. Retrieved from www.sociologysource.org/home/2012/5/22/speaking-in-class-is-always-optional.html

Patton, S. (2012). That's Dr. so-and-so to you. *The Chronicle of Higher Education*. Retrieved from www.chronicle.com/article/Thats-Dr-So-and-So-to-You/134226/

Pederson, L. (1965). Negro speech in *Adventures of Huckleberry Finn*. *Mark Twain Journal, 13*, 1–4.

Perryman-Clark, S. M. (2013). African American language, rhetoric, and students' writing: New directions for SRTOL. *College Composition and Communication, 64*, 469–495.

Peterson, S. (1984). *Down home and uptown: The representation of Black speech in American fiction*. Madison, NJ: Fairleigh Dickinson University Press.

Pierce, C. (1974). Psychiatric problems of the Black minority. In S. Arieti (Ed.), *American handbook of psychiatry* (pp. 512–523). New York: Basic Books.

Pinker, S. (2012). False fronts in the language wars. *Slate*. Retrieved from www.slate.com/articles/arts/the_good_word/2012/05/steven_pinker_on_the_false_fronts_in_the_language_wars_.html

Preston, J. (2012). If Twitter is a work necessity. *New York Times*. Retrieved from www.nytimes.com/2012/03/01/education/digital-skills-can-be-quickly-acquired.html

Purcell-Gates, V. (1997). *Other people's words: The cycle of low literacy*. Cambridge, MA: Harvard University Press.

Reaser, J. (2006). The effect of dialect awareness on adolescent knowledge and attitudes (doctoral dissertation). Duke University.

Reaser, J. L., & Wolfram, W. (2007). *Voices of North Carolina: Language and life from the Atlantic to the Appalachians*. Raleigh: North Carolina Language and Life Project.

Reed, J. S. (1986). *Southern folk plain and fancy: Native White social types*. Athens: University of Georgia Press.

Richardson, E. (2003a). Race, class(es), gender, and age: The making of knowledge about language diversity. In G. Smitherman & V. Villanueva (Eds.), *Language diversity in the classroom: From intention to practice* (pp. 40–66). Carbondale: Southern Illinois University Press.

Richardson, E. (2003b). *African American literacies*. New York: Routledge.

Richardson, E. (2009). My "ill" literacy narrative: Growing up Black, po and a girl, in the hood. *Gender and Education, 21*(6), 753–767.

Rickford, J. R., & Rickford, R. J. (2000). *Spoken soul: The story of Black English*. New York: Wiley.

Rickford, J. R., & Young, L. (2010, January). Sociolinguistic lessons in *A lesson before dying*. Presentation given to the American Dialect Society, Baltimore, MD.

Romaine, S. (1994). *Language in society: An introduction to sociolinguistics*. New York: Oxford University Press.

Romano, T. (1995). *Writing with passion: Life stories, multiple genres*. Portsmouth, NH: Boynton/Cook.

Royster, J. J. (1996). When the first voice you hear is not your own. *College Composition and Communication*, 47, 29–40.

Sadker, D., & Sadker, M. (1994). *Failing at fairness: How our schools cheat girls*. Toronto, ON: Simon & Schuster.

Sekaquaptewa, D., & Thompson, M. (2002). The differential effects of solo status on members of high and low status groups. *Personality and Social Psychology Bulletin, 28*, 694–707.

Shire, W. (2011). The birth name. *Warsan in wonderland*. Retrieved from www.diasporandarlings.com/interviews/warsan-shire-a-collection-of-inspiration

Singleton, G. E., & Linton, C. W. (2005). *Courageous conversations about race: A field guide for achieving equity in schools*. Thousand Oaks, CA: Corwin Press.

Skutnabb-Kangas, T. (1988). Multilingualism and the education of minority children. In O. García & C. Baker (Eds.), *Policy and practice in bilingual education: Extending the foundations* (pp. 40–62). Bristol, PA: Multilingual Matters.

Smith, A. (2011). Americans and text messaging. *The Pew Internet & American life project*. Retrieved from www.pewinternet.org/Reports/2011/Cell-Phone-Texting-2011/Main-Report/How-Americans-Use-Text-Messaging.aspx

Smitherman, G. (2000). *Talkin that talk: Language, culture, and education in African America*. New York: Routledge.

Smitherman, G., & Villanueva, V. (Eds.). (2003). *Language diversity in the classroom: From intention to practice*. Carbondale: Southern Illinois University Press.

Smithsonian. (2012). The first use of OMG was in a 1917 letter to Winston Churchill. Retrieved from http://blogs.smithsonianmag.com/smartnews/2012/11/the-first-use-of-omg-was-in-a-1917-letter-to-winston-churchill/

SparkNotes (2013). *No fear Shakespeare*. Retrieved from nfs.sparknotes.com/

Standing Bear, L. (1928). *My people the Sioux*. Lincoln, NE: University of Nebraska Press.

Steele, C. (2003). Stereotype threat and African-American student achievement. In T. Perry, C. Steele & A. Hilliard (Eds.), *Young, gifted, and Black: Promoting high achievement among African-American students* (pp. 109–130). Boston: Beacon Press.

Steele, C. M., & Aronson, J. (1995). Stereotype vulnerability and the intellectual test performance of African Americans. *Journal of Personality and Social Psychology*, *69*, 797–811.

Sue, D. W. (2010). *Microaggressions in everyday life: Race, gender, and sexual orientation*. New York: Wiley.

Sullivan, A. (2001). Cultural capital and educational attainment. *Sociology, 35*(4), 893–912.

Sullivan, A. (2007). Cultural capital, cultural knowledge and ability. *Sociological Research Online*, *12*(6). Retrieved from www.socresonline.org.uk/12/6/1.html

Tatum, B. D. (2007). Breaking the silence. In P. S. Rothenburg (Ed.), *White privilege* (3rd ed., pp. 147–152). New York: Worth Publishers.

Teaching Tolerance. (n.d.a). How to implement "Speak up at school." Retrieved from www.tolerance.org/activity/speak-school-how-respond-everyday-prejudice-bias

Teaching Tolerance. (n.d.b). *Speak up!* Retrieved from www.tolerance.org/publication/speak

Traugott, E. C. (1999). In fiction, whose speech, whose vision? In R. S. Wheeler (Ed.), *Language alive in the classroom* (pp. 167–177). Westport, CT: Praeger.

Trow, C. (2010). Give your college essay a voice. *NextStepU*. Retrieved from www.nextstepu.com/plan-for-college/college-admissions-essay/give-your-college-essay-a-voice.htm

Vendler, H. (2009). *Poems, poets, poetry: An introduction and anthology*. New York: Bedford/St. Martin's.

Verdi, G., & Ebsworth, M. E. (2009). Working-class women academics: Four sociolinguistic journeys. *Journal of Multicultural Discourses, 4*(2), 183–204.

Waitt, A. (2006). "A good story takes awhile": Appalachian literature in the high school classroom. *Journal of Appalachian Studies*, *12*(1), 79–101.

Wang, J., Iannotti, R. J., & Nansel, T. R. (2009). School bullying among adolescents in the United States: Physical, verbal, relational, and cyber. *Journal of Adolescent Health*, *45*(4), 368–375.

Warschauer, M. (2007). The paradoxical future of digital learning. *Learning Inquiry*, *1*(1), 41–49.

WikiHow (n.d.). How to email a professor. Retrieved from www.wikihow.com/Email-a-Professor

Williams, K. C. (2012). The role of instructors' sociolinguistic language awareness in college writing courses: A discourse analytic/ethnographic approach (doctoral dissertation). Georgetown University.

Wolfram, W. (1980). A-prefixing in Appalachian English. In W. Labov (Ed.), *Locating language in time and space* (pp. 107–142). New York: Academic Press.

Wolfram, W. (1998). Black children are verbally deprived. In L. Bauer & P. Trudgill (Eds.), *Language myths* (pp. 103–112). New York: Penguin.

Wolfram, W. (2000). Everyone has an accent. *Teaching Tolerance*. Retrieved from www.tolerance.org/magazine/number-18-fall-2000/everyone-has-accent

Wolfram, W., & Schilling-Estes, N. (2006). *American English* (2nd ed.). Malden, MA: Blackwell.

Wurr, A. J., & Hellebrandt, J. (2007). *Learning the language of global citizenship: Service-learning in applied linguistics*. Bolton, MA: Anker.

Zentella, A. C. (2005). *Building on strength: Language and literacy in Latino families and communities*. New York: Teachers College Press.

Zimmer, B. (2012). "Not to put too fine a point upon it": How Dickens helped shape the lexicon. *Visual Thesaurus*. Retrieved from www.visualthesaurus.com/cm/wordroutes/not-to-put-too-fine-a-point-upon-it-how-dickens-helped-shape-the-lexicon/

Selected Literary Texts

Novels, Short Stories, and Plays

Alcott, L. M. (1983). *Little women* (reprint ed.). New York: Bantam Classics.

Bambara, T. C. (2001). "The lesson." In *40 short stories: A portable anthology* (reprint ed.). Boston, MA: Bedford/St. Martin's.

Chaucer, G. (1986). *The Canterbury tales.* In *The Norton Anthology of English Literature* (reprint ed.). New York: Norton & Co.

Collier, J. L., & Collier, C. (1983). *War comes to Willy Freeman.* New York: Random House.

Dickens, C. (1996). *Bleak house* (reprint ed.). New York: Penguin Books.

Dickens, C. (2003). *David Copperfield* (reprint ed.). New York: Barnes & Noble.

Dickens, C. (1996) *Little Dorrit* (reprint ed.). Hertfordshire, UK: Wordsworth Editions Limited.

Ellison, R. (1990). *Invisible man* (reprint ed.). New York: Random House.

Faulkner, W. (1985). *As I lay dying* (reprint ed.). New York: Random House.

Faulkner, W. (1985). *Light in August* (reprint ed.). New York: Random House.

Fitzgerald, F. S. (2004). *The great Gatsby* (reprint ed.). New York: Scribner.

Fitzhugh, L. (2008). *Nobody's family is going to change* (reprint ed.). New York: Square Fish.

Gaines, E. (1993). *A lesson before dying.* New York: Alfred A. Knopf.

Golding, W. (1954). *Lord of the flies.* New York: Penguin Putnam Inc.

Hansberry, L. (1995). *A raisin in the sun* (reprint ed.). New York: Random House.

Hemingway, E. (1995). *For whom the bell tolls* (reprint ed.). New York: Scribner.

Hurston, Z. N. (1997). "Sweat." In *Spunk: The selected stories of Zora Neale Hurston.* Washington, DC: Marlowe & Co.

Hurston, Z. N. (1991). *Their eyes were watching God* (reprint ed.). Urbana: University of Illinois Press.

Jacobs, H. A. (2001). *Incidents in the life of a slave girl* (reprint ed.). New York: Dover Publications.

Johnson, S., & Johnson, A. D. (2010). *A ValueTales treasury: Stories for growing good people* (reprint ed.). New York: Simon & Schuster/Paula Wiseman Books.

Keene, C. (2006). *Nancy Drew complete series set* (reprint ed.). New York: Grosset & Dunlap.

Joyce, J. (2010). *Ulysses* (reprint ed.). Hertfordshire, UK: Wordsworth Editions Limited.

Lee, H. (2006). *To kill a mockingbird* (reprint ed.). New York: HarperCollins.
Lindgren, A. (2005). *Pippi Longstocking* (reprint ed.). New York: Puffin Modern Classics.
Mitchell, M. (2008). *Gone with the wind* (reprint ed.). New York: Pocket Books.
Montgomery, L. M. (2003). *Anne of green gables* (reprint ed.) New York: Signet Classics.
Morrison, T. (2004). *Beloved* (reprint ed.). New York: Alfred A. Knopf.
Morrison, T. (1970). *The bluest eye*. New York: Simon & Schuster.
Morrison, T. (1973). *Sula*. New York: Alfred A. Knopf.
O'Connor, F. (2000). "A good man is hard to find." In *The complete stories of Flannery O'Connor* (reprint ed.). New York: Farrar, Straus and Giroux.
O'Connor, F. (2000). "A stroke of good fortune." In *The complete stories of Flannery O'Connor* (reprint ed.). New York: Farrar, Straus and Giroux.
O'Connor, F. (2000). "Good country people." In *The complete stories of Flannery O'Connor* (reprint ed.). New York: Farrar, Straus and Giroux.
O'Connor, F. (2000). "The turkey." In *The complete stories of Flannery O'Connor* (reprint ed.). New York: Farrar, Straus and Giroux.
O'Connor, F. (2000). *Wise blood* (reprint ed.). New York: Farrar, Straus and Giroux.
Randall, D. (Ed.). (1985). *The Black poets* (reprint ed.). New York: Bantam.
Remarque, E. M. (1987). *All quiet on the Western front* (reprint ed.). New York: Ballantine Books.
Salinger, J. D. (1991). *The catcher in the rye* (reprint ed). New York: Little, Brown and Company.
Shakespeare, W. (1994). *Henry V*. In *The complete works of William Shakespeare*. New York: Barnes & Noble.
Shakespeare, W. (1994). *King Lear*. In *The complete works of William Shakespeare*. New York: Barnes & Noble.
Shakespeare, W. (1994). *Merchant of Venice*. In *The complete works of William Shakespeare*. New York: Barnes & Noble.
Shakespeare, W. (1994). *Much ado about nothing*. In *The complete works of William Shakespeare*. New York: Barnes & Noble.
Shakespeare, W. (1994). *Othello*. In *The complete works of William Shakespeare*. New York: Barnes & Noble.
Shakespeare, W. (1994). *The tempest*. In *The complete works of William Shakespeare*. New York: Barnes & Noble.
Shaw, G. B. (2005). *Pygmalion* (reprint ed.). New York: Simon & Schuster.
Steinbeck, J. (1993). *Grapes of wrath* (reprint ed.). New York: Penguin Books.
Steinbeck, J. (1993). *Of mice and men* (reprint ed.). New York: Penguin Books.
Stockett, K. (2009). *The help*. New York: Penguin Books.
Stowe, H. B. (2005). *Uncle Tom's cabin* (reprint ed.). New York: Dover Publications.
Taylor, M. D. (1991). *Roll of thunder, hear my cry* (reprint ed.). New York: Puffin Books.
Taylor, T. (2003). *The cay* (reprint ed.). New York: Random House.
Tolkien, J. R. R. (2012). *The hobbit* (reprint ed.). New York: Random House.
Toole, J. K. (1996). *A confederacy of dunces* (reprint ed.). New York: Wings Books.
Twain, M. (2008). *Adventures of Huckleberry Finn* (reprint ed.). New York: Barnes & Noble.

Twain, M. (2008). *The adventures of Tom Sawyer* (reprint ed.). New York: Barnes & Noble.
Vonnegut, K. (1991). *Slaughterhouse five* (reprint ed.). New York: Random House.
Walker, A. (2003). *The color purple* (reprint ed.). Orlando, FL: Mariner Books.

Poetry

Beowulf. Retrieved from http://www.fordham.edu/halsall/basis/beowulf-oe.asp
Cullen, C. "Incident."
Cummings, E. E. "you shall above all things be glad and young."
Cummings, E. E. "anyone lived in a pretty how town."
Cummings, E. E. "since feeling is first."
Donne, J. "Death be not proud."
Dunbar, P. L. "A Negro love song."
Dunbar, P. L. "I continue to dream."
Ellis, T. S. "All their stanzas look alike."
Ellis, T. S. "The genuine Negro hero."
Hughes, L. "Theme for English B."
Hughes, L. "Mother to son."
Lyon, G. E. "Where I'm from."
Milton, J. "Paradise lost."

Index

About the Authors

Anne H. Charity Hudley is associate professor of Education, English, Linguistics, and Africana Studies and the William & Mary Professor of Community Studies at the College of William & Mary in Williamsburg, Virginia. She also directs the William & Mary Scholars Program and codirects the William & Mary Scholars Undergraduate Research Experience (WMSURE). Her research and publications address the relationship between English language variation and K–16 educational practices and policies. Charity Hudley has served as a consultant to the National Research Council Committee on Language and Education and to the National Science Foundation's Committee on Broadening Participation in the Science, Technology, Engineering, and Mathematics (STEM) sciences. She is associate editor of *Language,* with specific responsibilities for *Teaching Linguistics,* a series of articles concerning the teaching of linguistics, and is on the editorial boards of *American Speech* and the sociolinguistics division of *Language and Linguistics Compass.* She has worked with K–12 educators through lectures and workshops sponsored by the American Federation of Teachers and by public and independent schools throughout the country.

Dr. Charity Hudley earned a BA and an MA in Linguistics from Harvard University in 1998. She was awarded a Ford Pre-Dissertation Fellowship in 2003. From 2003–2005 she was the Thurgood Marshall Dissertation Fellow at Dartmouth College. She earned a PhD in Linguistics from the University of Pennsylvania in 2005. She received a National Science Foundation Minority Postdoctoral Fellowship in fall 2005 and a National Science Foundation Minority Research Starter Grant in 2009.

Christine Mallinson is associate professor in the Language, Literacy, and Culture Program and affiliate associate professor in the Department of Gender and Women's Studies at the University of Maryland–Baltimore County (UMBC). Her research investigates the social contexts of English language variation, particularly with regard to region, ethnicity, social class, and gender. She has conducted extensive field research in Appalachia and throughout North Carolina, as well as in Washington, DC, and Baltimore, MD. Mallinson is associate editor of *American Speech*, coordinating the annual "Teaching

American Speech" pedagogical section, and she is the founder and moderator of the TeachLing online discussion group on linguistic pedagogy. She serves on the editorial board of the sociolinguistics division of *Language and Linguistics Compass* and is a member of the executive committee of the Southeastern Conference on Linguistics. She is also the coeditor of *Data Collection in Sociolinguistics: Methods and Applications* (2013).

Dr. Mallinson received a BA in sociology and German from the University of North Carolina at Chapel Hill in 2000, and an MA in English with a concentration in sociolinguistics from North Carolina State University in 2002. She received the Nancy G. Pollock Graduate School dissertation award for the College of Humanities and Social Sciences at North Carolina State University, where she earned a PhD in sociology and anthropology, with concentrations in sociolinguistics and social inequality, in 2006.

We Do Language is the authors' second book written for Teachers College Press. Their first book, *Understanding English Language Variation in U.S. Schools*, was published in 2011. Their current research, funded by the National Science Foundation, investigates how culturally and socially based language patterns affect teaching, learning, and student assessment in Science, Technology, Engineering and Mathematics (STEM) classrooms in the United States.